THE BIG SHIFT

REDEFINING MARKETING IN A MULTICULTURAL AMERICA

DR. JAKE BENIFLAH

Distribution by Bublish, Inc.

Paperback ISBN: 978-1-64704-223-3
eBook ISBN: 978-1-64704-221-9

CONTENTS

FOREWORD

There are dire predictions in this book for change-resistant business and marketing leaders. Ignore the narrative, numbers and nuances of a massive multicultural consumer transformation in America at your peril. Multiculturalism is leaving a profound mark on all aspects of life in America. From the selection of cosmetics, candy and condiments to preferences in the choice of TV-streaming, tattoos and take-outs.

It's not just the rapid growth, habits and attitudes of the 120 million pan-ethnic Americans of all colors and persuasions, but the new affinity, appeal and embrace of multi-cultural products by mainstream consumers of all ages, races and ethnicities. Intermarriage, cohabitation, cultural openness, receptivity and proximity have transformed the face of America and will continue to do so in the years ahead. The foreign-born population has more than quadrupled since the 1960s, while the percentage of foreign-born with European ancestry has dropped from 74% to 11%. The U.S.-born population of multicultural households has increased exponentially. The blending and mixing of races and ethnicities within households has become the norm for over half of the U.S. population under the age of 50. Fifty-three percent of the U.S. population is now under age 50 and lives in either multicultural households or households that are blended.

Brands can aggregate consumers regardless of race and ethnicity, as there is ample evidence to show they have the mindset, behavior and opportunity to think and buy outside of their root culture. Big, lucrative metro markets are becoming massively multicultural. Miami is 90 percent multicultural. Los Angeles is 73 percent blended. And New York, like many other immigrant cities, embodies a culturally diverse population that represents 68 percent of its residents. Brands will win or lose market share at the hyperlocal level. Here, they will need to understand and address what resonates with individual shoppers or households given the density and panoply of intermingled cultures that are shaping new buying considerations, preferences, behaviors and channels of purchase.

Maestros of multicultural consumerism will be embracing precision marketing technologies, hyper-efficient marketing practices and ever-smarter AI systems. They will need to unify and take action on insights from vast repositories of segmented shopper data, eCommerce transactions, Internet usage, social media activity, mobile device apps, media content consumption, and live, location-based intelligence.

This means rethinking, and maybe reinventing, product portfolios, branding campaigns, go-to-market strategies, and personalized engagement. And it will underscore the need for companies and marketing teams to become more diverse, culturally intuitive and adaptive on an organizational, operational and staffing level.

Donovan Neale-May, Executive Director, CMO Council
San Jose, CA., November 2020

PREFACE

L atino marketing books represent less than 1 percent of all marketing books in this country.[1] Less than 10 percent of all academic articles published in the top marketing journals focus on the U.S. Latino consumer.[2] And, only 45 percent of corporate CEOs recognize Latinos and other multicultural consumers as mission critical.[3] If corporations are to succeed in the 21st century, it is imperative that they understand how to win in the New Mainstream.

The Big Shift is a marketing book that places U.S. Latinos and other multicultural consumers at the center of corporate growth. The book is about marketing in a multicultural America. Its publication is planned to coincide with the release of the 2020 Census, which — if past Census releases are an indication — will generate tremendous interest by corporations, large and small. For those of us who've been in the marketing and advertising business long enough, we've seen this play out many times. New U.S. Census data present an opportunity for leading companies to ask whether they are doing enough to drive their business, and for followers and laggards to ask what more can they do to capitalize on the changing demographic landscape. The seismic shifts will require corporations across all sectors to rethink their marketing and organizational strategies with U.S. Latinos and other multicultural consumers, now and in the future. Companies that do not will suffer the consequences.

The Big Shift chronicles my 30 year journey in the U.S. mainstream and Latino advertising industry. This book is based on two research methodologies. The emic perspective, often referred to as an "insider's view," has allowed me to examine Latino marketing as a member of this tightly bound social group. By contrast, the etic perspective has given me the so-called "general market" angle on reaching Latino consumers, as an outsider looking in. This book benefits from these two complementary viewpoints, making it more objective and comprehensive.

This book answers some of the most pressing questions of our time: What will Latino marketing look like in the future? What direction should the industry take? Is Latino marketing a consumer-driven discipline or is it driven by an outdated business paradigm? What does in-culture marketing look like in a multicultural environment? There's no doubt in my mind that before we unleash the economic power of U.S. Latinos in the 21st century, we must shed all outdated perceptions and biases about marketing to this population.

The Big Shift is neither purely practitioner-driven nor purely academic. It is both. The book centers on a strategic framework designed to help marketers understand the trajectory of marketing to Latinos in the United States (where we were, where we are and where we need to go), and proposes fact-based, go-to-market solutions. This framework molds how the book is organized. Each chapter proposes significant change that corporations can no longer postpone or ignore. At its core, this book argues that corporations must make The Big Shift by placing Latinos and other multicultural consumers front and center of mainstream marketing as a way to drive growth in an increasingly diverse marketplace.

PREFACE ENDNOTES

[1] Estimates by the Center for Multicultural Science, 2020.

[2] Beniflah, J. and Chatterjee, S. (2015). An Epistemological Study of Hispanic Marketing, 1979–2015: The Need to Bridge Theory with Practice. *Journal of Cultural Marketing Strategy*. 1(1): 90-112.

[3] The CMO Council. (2015). Activating the New American Mainstream: Defining, Reaching and Engaging the Multicultural Market. The CMO Council. White Paper Series, September, 2015. Accessed on January 5, 2020: https://www.cmocouncil.org/thought-leadership/reports/activating-the-new-american-mainstream.

ACKNOWLEDGMENTS

*C*herchez la femme. I owe everything to my wife for her unconditional love and support, and a lifetime of encouragement. I'd like to thank my mother, mother-in-law, brother, sister, brothers-in-law, nephews and niece for their unyielding love. And my father, who passed away more than 10 years ago from pancreatic cancer, was by far the most courageous and compassionate individual I have known. Without my parents' sacrifices, my accomplishments would have been nothing but far-fetched dreams. Finally, my two sons, who are now 20 and 14, are my inspiration in writing this book.

I want to thank a number of colleagues who have supported me over my professional career: Brian Hughes, EVP and General Manager, Audience Intelligence and Strategy at MAGNA, for his friendship and industry leadership. Julie Veloz, Vice President, Global Diversity Intelligence & Strategy at Interpublic Group, for her thought leadership and vision. Dr. Sharmila Chatterjee, my former dissertation chair at Golden Gate University and currently the Academic Head for the MBA Track in Enterprise Management at MIT Sloan, for being an invaluable friend and advisor for almost two decades. Paul Fouts, my management professor at Golden Gate University, for his support and long conversations on organizational change. Dr. Jeffrey Huberman, Dean of the Slane College of Communication and Fine Arts at Bradley University, for his vision, leadership and support. And to Dr. Gerardo Marín, pioneer of acculturation measurement and my dissertation advisor, who passed away in 2017. He was an amazing scholar and friend.

I also want to thank all of the clients and colleagues with whom I worked throughout my career and to those with whom I spoke while writing this book. Thank you for your friendship and trust. This book was written for you and with you in mind. And to my editor, Laura Blum. Fate brought us together one afternoon in New York City. You are an incredible person, writer and dear friend. It was an honor sharing this journey with you. And to Lia Eristavi. You are the only person I trusted in designing the cover of this book. You are a remarkable friend and designer.

I dedicate this book to my wife, our respective parents and the estimated 45 million immigrants in this country.[4] I am one of them. The invaluable role we play in driving commerce and shaping the culture of this country will continue to make the United States a shining beacon to the world. Nobody, nothing will ever change that.

ACKNOWLEDGMENTS ENDNOTES

[4] U.S. Census Bureau. (2018). Current Population Survey, Annual Social and Economic Supplement. Accessed on January 10, 2020: https://www.census.gov/data/tables/2018/demo/foreign-born/cps-2018.html (Table 2.1. Foreign-Born Population by Sex, Age, and Year of Entry: 2018).

INTRODUCTION

Marketing in the United States is currently at a crossroads. The U.S. advertising and marketing industry is encountering an unprecedented inflection point spurred by the convergence of demographic and business forces that will require all corporations to reconfigure their marketing capabilities. Those that adapt will not only survive—but thrive. Those that don't will become obsolete and suffer the consequences. Corporations have two options: Follow the status quo and ignore change at the risk of monetizing the current business paradigm, which over time will lead to self-fulfilling failure, or adapt to the changing environment and develop new capabilities that can serve as the basis for self-fulfilling success (see Figure i).

The Big Shift outlines a strategic framework that brand marketers can use to successfully navigate through this inflection point and grow their business with U.S. Latinos and other multicultural consumers in the 21st century (see Figure ii). The proposed framework draws from the dynamic capabilities literature, which posits that companies must adapt, renew or reconfigure their current resources and capabilities to align with a changing competitive environment.[5] This alignment or strategic fit can be a source of a sustaining competitive advantage.[6] The framework identifies three forces — consumers, organizations and industry — that must align with a multicultural America.

Chapter 1 explores paradigms and paradigmatic change. It introduces the Hispanic Marketing Paradigm, a set of concepts and beliefs, including best practices, research methods and industry standards that have shaped marketing to U.S. Latinos for more than three decades. This chapter proposes that the Hispanic Marketing Paradigm is an outdated model and companies that do not make the sufficient and necessary changes are likely to face business declines.

Chapter 2 deals with the bicultural Latino. It is foundational to the framework. For more than 30 years, the Latino advertising and marketing industry (ad agencies, media publishers and trade associations) has depicted Latinos as a linguistically and culturally homogeneous niche segment. This is an oversimplification of U.S. Latinos. This chapter proposes that marketers must replace the aggregated, Spanish-language-centric view that has defined Latino marketing for decades with a broader, more nuanced approach that reflects the duality of the entire Latino population.[7]

Chapter 3 introduces the Nativity-Based View, a new media buying and planning methodology for U.S. Latinos.[8] Using data science, we found that nativity (not language) is a better predictor of what Latinos consume in media. Between 70 to 80 percent of Spanish-language linear television does not reach Latino Millennials, and an estimated $1 billion dollars have been misallocated in Spanish-language television attempting to reach this demographic.[9] The Nativity-Based View challenges the central notion that Spanish-language television is the "best way" to reach U.S. Latinos. This chapter can help brands drive media ROI.

Chapter 4 revisits in-culture marketing.[10] [11] Popularized in the early 1990s, it has served as the foundation in Latino marketing, unifying media publishers, measurement companies, advertising agencies, researchers and brand marketers. This chapter introduces two theoretical frameworks from social psychology, self-referencing and optimal distinctiveness theory, that help explain the drivers of in-culture marketing. This chapter can help brands improve creative effectiveness.

Chapter 5 looks at measurement. Traditionally, U.S. media ad spend has been aggregated and calculated by adding all consumers together. This chapter introduces the Ethnicity-Race View (ERV), a new measure that reports advertising spend by ethnicity and race.[12] As the mainstream reaches a multicultural tipping point, marketers will need to develop new measures to account for all segments of the population.

Chapters 6 and 7 examine mental models and leadership, and dynamic organizational capabilities, respectively. These chapters address important intra-organizational relationships. The link between mental models and organizational capabilities is a key part of the proposed framework, which helps address a number of issues that affect process and strategy within corporations. Both chapters suggest that corporations will need to make a shift in how they operate in order to achieve a strategic fit between their internal resources and capabilities and the opportunities in the external environment.[13] This internal transformation must be initiated by senior leadership, cascading across all levels of the organization.

Chapter 8 provides a vision for the future, a path forward. It synthesizes the external factors that shape marketing today (Chapters 1-5) and the organizational changes (Chapters 6-7) required to win in a multicultural America. Chapter 8 provides a number of general strategies for companies which are looking to grow with Latinos.

This book centers on corporate growth with U.S. Latinos. Some of the strategies and frameworks mentioned in this book can be applied to African American and other multicultural consumers based on how the advertising and marketing industry is currently structured. The unique differences within and among these groups are significant and require consumer-specific expertise. There are no shortcuts to success.

INTRODUCTION ENDNOTES

[5] Teece, D., Pisano, G., and Shuen, A. (1998). Dynamic Capabilities and Strategic Management. *Strategic Management Journal*. 18(7): 509-533.

[6] Porter, M. (1985). Competitive Advantage: Creating and Sustaining Superior Performance. New York: Free Press.

[7] Cortés-Vázquez, L., Montenegro, X., Willoth, S., Santiago, C., and Beniflah, J. (2014). Challenging the Belief that All U.S. Hispanics Are Culturally Homogeneous: An AHAA and AARP Cultural Orientation and Generational Study. *Journal of Brand Strategy*. 3(3): 235-244.

[8] Beniflah, J., Hughes, B., and Carrasco, M. (2018). Nativity-Based View: A New Audience Measurement Standard that Drives Television Return-On-Investment for U.S. Hispanics. *Journal of Cultural Marketing Strategy*. 3(1): 43-59.

[9] Ibid.

[10] Valdés, I. (2000). Marketing to American Latinos, Part 1. New York: Paramount Publishing.

[11] Valdés, I. (2002). Marketing to American Latinos, Part 2. New York: Paramount Publishing.

[12] Measuring media advertising spend by ethnicity and race was presented at The State of Video conference. March 4, 2019, New York City. The application of the ERV methodology on media ad spend was developed by The Center for Multicultural Science and MAGNA.

[13] Porter, M. E. (1979). How Competitive Forces Shape Strategy. *Harvard Business Review*. 57(2) March-April: 137-145.

Figure i
Inflection Point

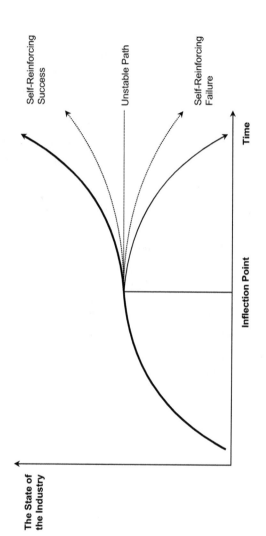

Source: The Center for Multicultural Science.

Figure ii
Strategic Framework

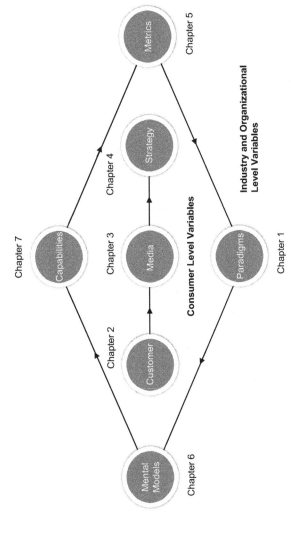

Source: The Center for Multicultural Science.

CHAPTER
ONE

This book proposes that corporations will need to make The Big Shift to win in a multicultural America. Understanding what companies are shifting from is critical to their success. In this chapter, I outline a distinct set of beliefs and research methods that helped launch Latino marketing more than 30 years ago. Drawing from Thomas Kuhn's seminal book, *The Structure of Scientific Revolutions*, I review the different phases of paradigm creation and change, and apply them to the discipline of Latino marketing. Kuhn's work serves as a conceptual model to help explain the paradigm that has governed the business of Latino marketing, which I have coined the Hispanic Marketing Paradigm.[14] This chapter provides an overview of: (1) the structure of paradigm formation and change; (2) the creation of the Hispanic Marketing Paradigm; and (3) the necessary shifts in marketing to help drive corporate growth in the 21st century.

BRIEF OVERVIEW OF KUHN

Thomas Kuhn, a physicist and University of California-Berkeley professor of the history of science, proposed the process by which major changes come about in scientific fields. He hypothesized that revolutions in science result from breakdowns in intellectual systems that occur when old research methods fail to solve new problems, rather than evolving gradually through steady and incremental inquiries by established researchers in a given discipline. He called the change that underlies this kind of revolution a paradigm shift.

Kuhn's thesis in *The Structure of Scientific Revolutions* centers on the notion that when a scientific field is going through a stable period, most of its practitioners hold a common set of beliefs and assumptions. They agree on the problems that need to be solved, the rules that govern research and the standards by which performance is measured. They share a conceptual model — or in Kuhn's parlance, a paradigm — that dictates the activities of observation, research and experimentation in a given sphere of specialization. Students and practitioners court membership in an intellectual community by embracing its reigning paradigm.

Kuhn also argued that paradigms aren't permanent. When practitioners encounter anomalies or phenomena that cannot be explained by the status quo model, the paradigm begins to show signs of instability. For a while, those who subscribe to the paradigm try to ignore the contradictions or inconsistencies that they find, or they make ad hoc changes to cope with immediate crises. Eventually, when enough anomalies accumulate to make a substantial number of researchers question the current paradigm, its challengers innovate a fresh one. If enough scientists become convinced that the new paradigm works better than the old one, they will accept it as the new norm. The replacement of one conceptual model by another is what Kuhn dubbed a paradigm shift. His book served up the classic example of substituting the Copernican model of the solar system for the Ptolemaic model and the development of Newtonian physics. Such shifts are often disorderly and controversial, and the period in which they develop is marked by insecurity and conflict within the discipline.

Kuhn believed that, because these shifts are so disruptive, they will occur only when the number of unsolved problems reaches a crisis point, and leading practitioners begin to focus on these unsolved problems. Even with mounting evidence that the conceptual model doesn't work, supporters of the traditional paradigm resist change because they have an intellectual, emotional and financial investment in the accepted view. Over time, resistance to the new paradigm lessens as advocates demonstrate that it solves problems the traditional paradigm cannot. Most of the iconoclasts adopt a new model and their more traditional colleagues gradually come to accept it. Those who cling to the old paradigm lose their influence in the field because the vanguard simply ignored their work. When that happens, the paradigm shift is complete and the theory that was once revolutionary becomes conventional.

HISPANIC MARKETING PARADIGM

Paradigms are essential to scientific inquiry. "No natural history can be interpreted in the absence of at least some implicit body of intertwined theoretical and methodological belief that permits selection, evaluation, and criticism," Kuhn observed.[15] As he saw it, paradigms begin with the creation of avenues of inquiry in which a random collection of facts are gathered to help a scientific community explain some specific phenomena. During these early stages of inquiry, different researchers confronting the same phenomenon describe and interpret it in divergent ways. This "pre-paradigmatic" period features a number of schools vying for preeminence. Out of the competition among pre-paradigmatic schools, a paradigm finally emerges.

According to Kuhn, "To be accepted as a paradigm, a theory must seem better than its competitors."[16] Eight decades into the 20th century, a new paradigm in Latino marketing provided the scientific community with a set of core beliefs that allowed it to practice its trade. These new beliefs formed the foundation of educating and preparing researchers in the field. From its earliest days, the business of Latino marketing marched to a strict set of paradigmatic rules that would harden into dogma. This Hispanic Marketing Paradigm is based on five socially constructed marketing principles: (1) Latinos are the largest and among the fastest-growing ethnic segments in the country; (2) they have a preference for speaking Spanish over English; (3) in-language media is the "best way" to reach them; (4) ethnic ad agencies have the unparalleled expertise over general market ad agencies to understand multicultural consumers; and (5) brand marketers need to fund Latino marketing efforts separately from mainstream marketing. These five edicts of the Hispanic Marketing Paradigm made U.S. Latino marketing a billion-dollar business (see Figure 1).

The concept of a scientific community is fundamental to the concept of a paradigm. In the Hispanic Marketing Paradigm, the scientific community is comprised of a number of stakeholders, Spanish-language media, Latino advertising agencies, measurement organizations and research companies, that have individually and collectively played a role to establish and reinforce the rules governing U.S. Latino marketing. Brand marketers, the beneficiaries of this paradigm, helped popularize the principles that impelled the Hispanic Marketing Paradigm. By 1996, the first Latino marketing trade association, the Association of Hispanic Advertising Agencies (now called Culture Marketing Council) was launched. This helped amplify the Hispanic Marketing Paradigm. Latino marketing courses sprung up in universities across the country; publishers cranked out textbooks and business primers; and symposiums and conferences filled halls. This new marketing discipline was established as a silo, an extension of the mainstream that posed little threat to mainstream marketing.

Fundamentally, paradigm-based research is "an attempt to force nature into a preformed and relatively inflexible box that the paradigm supplies," [17] as Kuhn put it. No effort is made to call forth new phenomena or discover anomalies. And when anomalies pop up, they're usually discarded or ignored. The Hispanic Marketing Paradigm conceptualized Latinos as culturally and linguistically homogeneous, which helped differentiate them from non-Latino Whites. (It is common knowledge that the U.S. Latino population is diverse and comprised of many countries around the world.) Nevertheless, the Hispanic Marketing Paradigm was designed to aggregate the intra-cultural differences of U.S. Latinos, constructing a pan-ethnic segment with generalized cultural similarities that were easy for brand marketers to understand. [18]

Language is at the epicenter of the Hispanic Marketing Paradigm. Latinos are characterized as preferring Spanish over English, and exhibiting an emotional response to in-language advertising (i.e., Share of Heart). [19] The Nielsen language quintiles are an example of how syndicated research and media measurement companies helped shape the Hispanic Marketing Paradigm from the get-go. The language quintiles measure language-use-at-home across five levels: (1) Spanish only; (2) more Spanish than English; (3) about the same; (4) more English than Spanish; and (5) English only. Although language is just one variable in culture, the Hispanic Marketing Paradigm made it its core. Spanish was not only used to define the U.S. Latino population, it defined U.S. Latino marketing.

This language-centric paradigm fueled the in-language media industry with linear television making up the overwhelming majority of ad spend.

In addition to language, focusing on the cultural differences between Latinos and non-Latinos helped justify different marketing approaches. In-culture marketing is a methodology that uncovers unique cultural factors that help explain consumer behavior.[20] [21] This approach helped an entire industry target Latinos in-language with culturally relevant insights. Much of the work perpetuating the Hispanic Marketing Paradigm was instrumental in the industry's growth. Kuhn called this normal science, and "mopping up" is what normal science is all about. It's the activity that keeps most scientists engaged throughout their entire careers, compressing reality into inflexible boxes or silos that help define the paradigm. In the end, paradigms gain their status by being more successful than their competitors in solving problems that the group of practitioners has come to recognize as acute.

One of the things the scientific community acquires with a paradigm is the criterion for choosing the problems it plans to solve. The assurance that the question has an answer *is* the criterion. Researchers who strive to solve problems defined by the existing paradigm aren't just looking around. The paradigm frames the objectives of their research, the methodology and instruments to be used and even guides the thoughts researchers entertain about normal science. Paradigms are powerful. But what happens when a few researchers call out specific anomalies as dire, threatening the Hispanic Marketing Paradigm?

Research and researchers with whom the scientific community disagrees are alienated from the industry. If new research does not align with a paradigm (i.e., the Hispanic Marketing Paradigm), its tenets are criticized and rejected, and avenues used to disseminate new phenomena and research are closed off. It's critical to the viability of a paradigm that no outliers or anomalies interfere with the writs regulating its discipline. Change, therefore, is the real enemy to any paradigm because it threatens its normal science.

If normal science is rigid and its scientific communities are close-knit, how do paradigms ever change? The first step towards change converges on the discovery of an anomaly, the recognition that nature has violated the paradigm-induced expectations driving normal science. It's important to note that discovery involves an extended process of conceptual assimilation, yet integrating new information doesn't always lead to paradigm change. Kuhn even acknowledged that, "Not all theories are paradigm theories." The emergence of a new theory is generated by the persistent failure of normal science to solve increasingly pressing puzzles. Failure of the existing rules is the prelude to the search for new ones.

THE PROPOSED SHIFTS

Today, U.S. Latino marketing is facing a slow existential crisis for more than a decade. This crisis has been driven by the "total market" advertising approach.[22] General market agencies are one-stop shops for many brands, replacing the valuable work of ethnic marketing agencies. The one-size-fits-all approach driven by non-Latino White consumers is dated and off-strategy. This new industry structure excludes the specialization of Latino and other multicultural agencies at a time when brands need them most. Total market hurts brands in a multicultural America because there *are* better models out there.

So, what should marketers do? The paradigm behind marketing needs to move in step with the demographic, media and technological changes impacting the business landscape. A new generation of workers with different lived experiences and perspectives is apt to view marketing differently. A critical factor in the proposed shift is the willingness of corporate America to leverage talent who are subject-matter experts and hold a specialization with the New Mainstream. Segregating the business by ethnicity, race and language is an outdated 20th-century paradigm. The convergence of the U.S. demographic landscape will require greater collaboration and integration across teams within and across brands and their advertising agencies. Structure will precede strategy.[23]

I have proposed a number of changes that can help corporations drive marketing effectiveness in today's diverse landscape: (1) integrate and elevate Latinos and other multicultural consumers into a brand's overall growth strategy; (2) challenge the cultural and linguistic homogeneity of Latinos and embrace the full diversity and duality of the Latino cohort; (3) rethink the media preferences of Latinos and reject the notion that the single "best way" to reach them is with in-language media; (4) place U.S. Latinos front and center of the new mainstream; and (5) rightsize media investments commensurately.

In closing, the pioneers and industry leaders who created Latino marketing and worked tirelessly to position Latinos as a key growth segment deserve tremendous credit. The seeds they planted decades ago have helped the ad industry reap significant financial rewards. More than three decades later, however, the Hispanic Marketing Paradigm no longer serves marketers well. But neither does the "total market" approach. We owe corporate America new thinking and a more effective strategy that reflects a 21st-century marketplace. This is what the rest of the book will focus on.

Figure 1
The Hispanic Marketing Paradigm

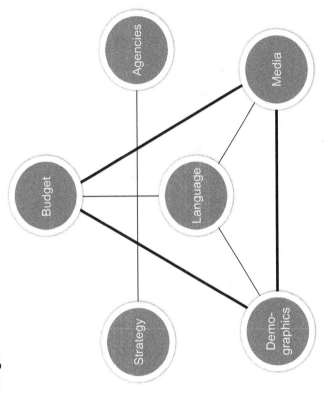

Source: The Center for Multicultural Science.

CHAPTER ONE ENDNOTES

[14] Beniflah, J., Hughes, B., and Garcia, C. (2015). Paradigm Shift: The Effect of Nativity and Years-In-Country on Television Programming Viewing Across Three Hispanic Generational Levels. *Journal of Cultural Marketing Strategy.* 1(1): 19-31.

[15] Kuhn, T. (1962). The Structure of Scientific Revolutions. Chicago: The University of Chicago Press, page 28.

[16] Ibid, page 17.

[17] Ibid, page 24.

[18] Dávila, A. (2001). Latinos Inc.: The Marketing and Making of a People. Berkeley: University of California Press.

[19] Valdés, I. (2008). Hispanic Customers for Life: A Fresh Look at Acculturation. New York: Paramount Publishing.

[20] Valdés, I. (2000). Marketing to American Latinos, Part 1. New York: Paramount Publishing.

[21] Valdés, I. (2002). Marketing to American Latinos, Part 2. New York: Paramount Publishing.

[22] Miller, P. (2013). Total Market Gets Lots of Buzz, But Multicultural Agencies Will Suffer Badly. *AdAge.* Accessed on January 22, 2020: https://adage.com/article/the-big-tent/total-market-shoves-multicultural-agencies/245657

[23] Porter, M. (1985). Competitive Advantage: Creating and Sustaining Superior Performance. New York: Free Press.

CHAPTER
TWO

Marketing is defined as a set of activities that drive organizational value through the customer.[24] This chapter centers on the U.S. bicultural Latino, who rightfully sits at the heart of our strategic framework. For decades, the conceptualization of U.S. Latinos has been oversimplified.[25] This chapter challenges the Hispanic Marketing Paradigm by disaggregating the Latino population. In this chapter, I introduce a practical, two-tier conceptual framework based on nativity and acculturation that allows brands in any category to better understand and market to the diverse Latino population. It is a model into which any variable can be placed to drive growth. This chapter examines: (1) the cultural differences and similarities between Latinos and other population segments in the U.S., using Hofstede's global cultural values framework and (2) measures the cultural orientation of U.S. Latinos and non-Latino Whites based on a Bicultural Involvement Questionnaire. Commonly referred to as BIQ, this questionnaire yields two independent measures of language use and cultural involvement in the United States. In this chapter, I challenge the notion that Latinos are culturally homogeneous as suggested by the Hispanic Marketing Paradigm and propose that it is more accurate for brands to redefine U.S. Latinos by their cultural duality.

CONCEPTUAL FRAMEWORK

Targeting U.S. Latinos in Spanish has defined Latino marketing for more than 30 years, creating what is today a multibillion-dollar industry. This is a feat few could have ever imagined back in the late 1980s and 1990s. More than three decades later, the two-tier framework proposed in this chapter supplants language as the dominant variable in marketing to Latinos in the 21st century. The relationship between language and thought has been well-established since the turn of the century,[26-29] but the notion that Spanish defines Latinos in the United States aligns more with an industry narrative rather than with the Latino population. A more accurate conceptual framework envisions language as a variable within Latino marketing and not as the driver of its business. This is a critical, foundational shift in helping brands optimize targeting effectiveness and media ROI with Latinos.

The two-tier framework is a simple yet powerful mechanism that produces insights for brands (see Figure 2). Nativity can be conceptualized in a number of ways, but the proposed model is based on how nativity is defined by the U.S. Census. The U.S. Census Bureau uses the term "generational status" (i.e., nativity) to refer to the place of birth of an individual or an individual's parents. Questions about place of birth and parental place of birth are used to define the first, second and third+ generations. The first generation refers to those who are foreign born. Those who are born in the United States with at least one foreign-born parent or with two foreign-born parents represent the second generation. That leaves the third+ generation, which includes those who are born in the United States with two U.S. native parents. Cultural attachment to one's native country has a significant impact on a whole host of variables — everything from attitudes and cognition to cultural values and consumption. As such, nativity represents a more impactful variable, helping marketers identify key segments and characteristics of U.S. Latinos.

The secondary dimension of the framework is acculturation. Acculturation deals with social and psychological change in which there is continuous contact and interaction among individuals of different cultures.[30] These changes can be observed across domains ranging from attitudes, values and behaviors to a sense of cultural identity.[31] [32] Although the changes implied in this definition can affect either or all of the groups involved (i.e., the culture rating for the dominant cultural group), most studies regarding acculturation seem to capture changes that occur in the group and individuals who are acculturated to a dominant culture.[33] The classic definition also implies that acculturation is an interactive, developmental and multidimensional process.[34] The measurement of acculturation, however, is a bit more complicated and subtle. There are linear acculturation models that are easy to implement, but limited in what they can measure.[35] Bidimensional models, on the other hand, are more nuanced in what they measure, but are lengthy and may present feasibility issues.[36] Single-proxy measures of acculturation (such as language) are unreliable and should be used with caution.[37] This is an important point because marketers in the U.S. continue to use language as a proxy for acculturation.

Our proposed framework assesses changes within the U.S Latino population across three generational levels. The framework is based on a bidimensional model measuring acculturation across two cultural domains: Latino and American. It does not support the zero-sum assumptions of linear acculturation, which presuppose that the adoption of a host country comes at the expense of one's native country.[38] The construct of acculturation in our framework tracks two cultures simultaneously. This is the most accurate and complete way of understanding the differences and similarities of Latinos living in the United States.

For first-generation Latinos, the level of acculturation to American life is low.[39] Their understanding of and resonance with American culture lag compared to their second- and third-generation Latino counterparts.[40] First-generation Latinos (all of whom are foreign born) have a high proficiency in Spanish and rely on the Latino culture as a reference point to make sense of their new cultural surroundings.[41] Over time, they begin to adopt more of the host country's ways as their level of cultural familiarity increases.[42] Second-generation Latinos, all of whom are native born, grow up speaking Spanish and English and code-switch throughout their lives.[43] They self-identify as Latino, live in two cultural domains and consume content across a number of media platforms spanning digital, social, OTT and linear television.[44] On the other hand, third-generation Latinos are also U.S. born, but are English-dominant and the most acculturated segment of all Latinos.

The following section of this chapter presents key findings of an important study comparing all U.S. multicultural segments based on Hofstede's six dimensions of national culture. Contrary to popular belief, the results show a considerable level of convergence in cultural values between Latinos and other segments of the U.S. population.[45] Specifically, Latinos were not found to be all that different across a number of cultural values when compared to U.S. non-Latino Whites, Asians and African Americans.[46] This finding challenges the widespread and long-held belief that Latinos possess different cultural values from U.S. non-Latinos and other multicultural groups.[47]

U.S. CULTURAL VALUES STUDY

Cross-cultural research acknowledges that individuals living in different societies diverge in their cultural values.[48] [49] According to Hofstede, culture is "the collective programming of minds that distinguishes the members of one group or category of people from others."[50] Similarly, other scholars have described culture as shared motives, values, beliefs, identities and interpretations or meanings of significant events that result from common experiences of members of collectives and are transmitted across age generations.[51] Given that cultures vary in terms of values, it's important for marketers to understand cross-cultural variation in values to determine the appropriateness of marketing and advertising strategies.[52]

Hofstede developed a model of six dimensions of national culture that helps explain basic value differences.[53] The six cultural dimensions are: Power Distance (PDI); Individualism (IDV); Masculinity (MAS); Uncertainty Avoidance (UAI); Long-Term orientation (LTO) and Indulgence (IND).[54] These dimensions are measured on a scale from 0 to 100. The model is based on quantitative research and gives scores for 75 countries and regions. In the second edition of his book *Culture's Consequences*, Hofstede described more than 200 external comparative studies and replications that have supported his indexes.[55] The dimensions can be used to explain differences in people's needs and motives, communication styles, language structure and metaphors and concepts used in advertising across different countries.[56] A brief description of each cultural dimension follows:

Power Distance Index (PDI): The Power Distance Index is defined as "the extent to which the less powerful members of organizations and institutions (like the family) accept and expect that power is distributed unequally."[57] In this dimension, inequality and power are perceived by the lower strata, or the followers. A higher index mark indicates that hierarchy is clearly established and executed in society, without doubt or reason. A lower index mark signifies that people question authority and attempt to distribute power.

Individualism vs. Collectivism (IDV): This index explores the degree to which people in a society are integrated into groups.[58] Individualistic societies have loose ties that often only relate an individual to his/her immediate family. They emphasize the "I" versus the "we." Individualism's counterpart, collectivism, describes a society in which tightly integrated relationships tie extended families and others into in-groups. These in-groups are undoubtedly loyal to family and support each other when a conflict arises with another in-group.

Uncertainty Avoidance (UAI): The Uncertainty Avoidance Index is defined as "a society's tolerance for ambiguity,"[59] in which people embrace or avert something unexpected, unknown or deviating from the status quo. Societies that score a high degree in this index opt for stiff codes of behavior, guidelines and laws, and generally subscribe to absolute truth, or to the belief that one lone truth dictates everything, and people know what it is. A lower degree in this index shows more acceptance of differing thoughts or ideas. In a society that tends to impose fewer regulations, ambiguity is more tolerated, and the environment is freer flowing.

Masculinity vs. Femininity (MAS): In this dimension, masculinity is defined as "a preference in society for achievement, heroism, assertiveness and material rewards for success."[60] Its counterpart represents "a preference for cooperation, modesty, caring for the weak and quality of life."[61] Women in these respective societies tend to display different values. In feminine societies, they share modest and caring views equally with men. In more masculine societies, women are somewhat assertive and competitive, but notably less than men. In other words, they still recognize a gap between male and female values. This dimension is frequently viewed as taboo in highly masculine societies.

Long-Term Orientation vs. Short-Term Orientation (LTO): This dimension addresses how different countries relate to the past, present and future. A lower ranking on this index (short-term) indicates that traditions are honored and kept, and steadfastness is valued. Societies with a high ranking (long-term) view adaptation and circumstantial, pragmatic problem-solving as a necessity. A country that is oriented toward the short-term usually has little to no economic development, whereas countries with a long-term orientation continue to develop.

Indulgence vs. Restraint (IND): This dimension refers to the degree of freedom that societal norms give citizens in fulfilling their human desires. Hofstede defined Indulgence as, "a society that allows relatively free gratification of basic and natural human desires related to enjoying life and having fun."[62] Its opposite number, per Hofstede, is "a society that controls gratification of needs and regulates it by means of strict social norms."[63]

In 2016, I had the privilege of working and publishing a study with Marieke de Mooij in the *Journal of International Consumer Marketing*.[64] We applied Hofstede's VSM (Values Survey Module) methodology to a number of ethnic groups in the U.S. Our goal was to determine the degree to which within-group differences existed across six cultural dimensions. It was the first of its kind. We produced matched samples for Mexican

Americans, Latinos of Cuban origin, Latinos of Puerto Rican descent, African Americans, Chinese Americans and non-Latino Whites. Geometry Global, a global shopper-marketing agency, sponsored the data collection and recruitment of a sample of 1,400 respondents: 200 U.S. Latinos (Cuban); 200 U.S. Latino (Mexican); 200 U.S. Latino (Puerto Rican); 200 U.S. Asian (Chinese); 300 African American and 300 non-Latino Whites. For each of these cultural groups, the following variables were measured: age (18-34, 35-49); nativity (U.S. born, foreign born); gender (male, female); income ($25,000-$49,999 and $50,000-$75,000); education (high school graduate/some college) and employment (part time/full time).

The study's most interesting finding was that the values of the various ethnic groups in the United States (except for Chinese Americans) substantially overlap with those of non-Latino Whites in the U.S.[65] This was demonstrated by the relatively small differences between the dimension scores of the various ethnic groups (see Table 2) and the national levels of nations (see Table 2.1).[66] As found in other studies, African Americans scored as individualistic as non-Latino Whites.[67] [68] In fact, all groups in our study scored individualistic and low on power distance. Our study did not confirm the conventional wisdom among marketers that U.S. Latinos are collectivistic compared to non-Latino Whites. In fact, only Chinese Americans scored significantly lower on individualism. All groups scored relatively high on the masculinity-femininity dimension, which conforms to the scores of the countries of origin. African Americans scored lowest on uncertainty avoidance, with Cuban Americans scoring highest. All groups scored low on long- vs. short-term orientation, to the surprise of the Chinese Americans, who typically score high on this value. Yet, this segment scored lowest on indulgence vs. restraint (IVR), which points to the original Chinese value of thrift. Mexican Americans scored highest on IVR, which reflects the values of their country of origin, Mexico.

Table 2.2 outlines the cultural dimension scores between U.S.-born and foreign-born Latinos and Chinese Americans, and Table 2.3 reports cultural scores by age.[69] [70] In summary, nativity matters when comparing cultural values across groups within the United States. In several cases, a relationship with the country of origin can be found among the older demographic, which may signal the effects of acculturation within a group. Analysis of the two age groups reveals that Millennials across the various ethnic groups are not more similar to each other than the elder groups.[71] Contrary to our expectations, no clear pattern emerged.[72] There were a few striking findings, such as young African Americans who scored higher than their elders on all dimensions, while young Chinese Americans scored lower than their senior counterparts.[73] For the three Latino groups, the results were more diffuse.[74] The cultural dimension scores among groups in the United States (i.e., Latinos, African Americans, Asians and non-Latino Whites) suggest that there's no uniform cultural pattern for multicultural consumers in the U.S. and that country of origin and ethnic and racial differences and similarities do exist, simultaneously.[75] No single pattern, however, described any one group across all the dimensions of culture, and no accurate cultural generalizations could be made.[76]

The study was conducted with the general hypothesis that ethnic and racial groups in the United States differ across all cultural dimensions. After all, they self-ascribe to different races and ethnicities. So naturally we expected differences to emerge among groups. This was not the case. The data were inconclusive, with some ethnic groups converging on some cultural dimensions while other groups diverged on others.[77] This may suggest that ethnic consumers in the United States are not as different as they've been made out to be by marketing professionals.

The main takeaway of our study is that culture is not necessarily a zero-sum game: Some ethnic groups in the United States diverge on some cultural dimensions and diverge on others.[78] Interestingly, the findings of our study affirm a long-held principle that Hofstede's research has made for decades: There is generally less cultural diversity within a nation than across nations.[79-82] It's possible that cultural differences in the United States exist because it's a country of immigrants from diverse nations around the world. This may explain why our research found divergence on some cultural dimensions. For those groups whose cultural values showed minimal differences, the trend of cultural convergence can be explained by the fact that they tend to reside in one country where they live and work side-by-side.

U.S. CULTURAL ORIENTATION STUDY

Today, marketers consider Millennials a coveted segment of the Latino population. They make up 29 percent of all Latinos and are characterized by their ability to speak in two languages and live in two cultures.[83] But is this true for just Millennials? Or do other segments within the Latino population also exhibit a sense of cultural duality?

In the following section, I plan to unpack the cultural orientation of Latinos across three cohorts (Millennials, Gen Xers and Boomers) and show how nativity and acculturation affect the degree to which Latinos adopt different dimensions of the Latino and U.S. cultures. The findings in this section can help organizations develop a more nuanced bidimensional view of all Latino consumers. Acculturation reflects a complex set of attitudinal and behavioral changes that individuals undergo when they sustain contact with members of a host (dominant) social group (U.S.).[84] These changes can be observed across a number of domains, such as attitudes, values, behaviors and a sense of cultural identity.[85] Cultural orientation, on the other hand, can be defined as the degree to which individuals actively engage in the traditions, values and practices of a specific culture.[86]

Published in a special issue of the *Journal of Brand Strategy* entitled "Multicultural Marketing," a study examined the differences and similarities of three Latino generational segments: Millennials (18-29 years); Gen Xers (30-44 years) and Boomers (45-65 years).[87] The study recruited 1,200 respondents (900 Latinos and 300 non-Latinos). It utilized a proxy acculturation scale (PAS-3) to measure acculturation, comprised of three factors: language of interview, language spoken at home and proportion of life lived in the U.S.[88] The model was coded using a five-point scale, ranging from Spanish only to English only. The higher the score, the greater the acculturation level. Despite the limitations of unidimensional acculturation models, the Cronbach's alpha for the PAS-3 is high at 0.79. (For more information on the PAS-3, refer to Cruz, *et al.*).[89]

This study, entitled *Challenging the Belief that All U.S. Hispanics Are Culturally Homogeneous: An AHAA and AARP Cultural Orientation and Generational Study*,[90] utilized the Bicultural Involvement Questionnaire (BIQ).[91] This oft-cited BIQ yields two independent measures of language use and cultural involvement reflecting a respondent's orientation to both U.S. culture (Americanism) and Hispanic culture (Hispanicism). Responses to all 33 items are scored on a scale of 1-5, with higher scores denoting greater orientation to the target culture or language (i.e., American). The Cronbach's alphas for these two subscales are high at 0.93 (Hispanicism) and 0.89 (Americanism).

The BIQ is comprised of two subscales: the American Cultural Orientation Scale (ACOS) and the Hispanic Cultural Orientation Scale (HCOS). The ACOS can be obtained by adding all of the items reflecting an involvement in U.S. culture (6-I0, 21-30 and 31-37). The lowest possible score in this scale is 22 (where a respondent scores all 1s), and the maximum score is 110 (a respondent scores all 5s). (For more information on how the BIQ is coded, refer to Szapocznik, *et al*.)[92] Our cultural orientation study produced three important findings, directly challenging the Hispanic Marketing Paradigm.[93]

Finding #1: As shown in Table 2.4, the mean score for the HCOS was lowest among Latino Millennials and Boomers (both 3.5) and highest among Gen Xers (3.7). Conversely, the mean score for the ACOS dipped most among Gen Xers (3.6) and peaked among Millennials (3.8) and Boomers (3.7). These findings suggest that a level of cultural duality exists across all Latino generational segments, not exclusively among Millennials or the main segments of the Latino population. Despite the close mean scores, t-tests revealed significant differences between select Latino generational groups (Latino Millennials and Boomers) across the ACOS and HCOS. No significant differences were found across ACOS and HCOS for Latino Gen Xers. (See Cortés-Vásquez, *et al.*, for details).[94]

Finding #2: The study found that the cultural orientation of Latinos varied significantly across three acculturation levels. Based on t-tests shown in Table 2.5, the mean score for the ACOS was lowest among low-acculturated Latinos (3.2) and highest among high-acculturated Latinos (4.2). Inversely, the mean score for the HCOS was most elevated among low-acculturated Latinos (4.1) and least among high-acculturated Latinos (3.1). HCOS and ACOS were relatively similar for moderately-acculturated Latinos (3.8 and 4.0, respectively). The study found statistically significant differences between ACOS and HCOS for low- and high-acculturated Latinos only. The mean score difference between ACOS and HCOS among moderately-acculturated Latinos was not statistically significant at the 95 percent confidence level. (See Cortés-Vásquez, *et al.*, for details).[95]

Finding #3: The study found significant differences in cultural orientation by nativity across three generational Latino segments (Millennials, Gen Xers and Boomers). As shown in Table 2.6, the mean score differences for ACOS and HCOS varied significantly between U.S.-born and foreign-born Latinos across Millennials, Gen Xers and Boomers. In addition, the mean score for Latino cultural orientation was higher for foreign-born Latinos regardless of the generational level (4.0, 4.0, 3.9), while the mean score for Anglo cultural orientation was found to be lower for foreign-born Latinos (3.5, 3.3 and 3.4). For U.S.-born Latinos, the patterns were just the opposite: Mean scores for ACOS were higher (4.1, 4.1, 4.1) than those for HCOS (3.3, 3.2, 3.2) across all three generational segments (Millennials, Gen Xers, Boomers, respectively). The analysis of variance tests showed statistically significant differences at the 95 percent confidence level when comparing mean scores between HCOS and ACOS for foreign-born and U.S.-born Latinos across Millennials, Gen Xers and Boomers. (See Cortés-Vásquez, *et al.*, for details).[96]

This study bears several noteworthy implications. First, our study found significant differences in cultural orientation across three Latino generations. This is significant because it refutes the current orthodoxy that all U.S. Latinos are culturally homogeneous. The study substantiates the notion that generational marketing can help corporations target the optimal Hispanic customer, and it additionally points up why deciphering cultural orientation among Latinos can enhance marketing effectiveness for corporations.

The second major benefit of this study centers on the use of cultural orientation as a complement to existing acculturation models. While most acculturation models are based on proxy variables, which do not measure aspects of culture, such cultural-orientation scales as the BIQ can help marketers explore dimensions of culture (notably cultural orientation), where important consumer insights can be used to steer more effective marketing strategies.

Third, this study sheds light on a bankable truth: There's no single "best way" to target the U.S. Latino consumer. As shown in the study, Latinos differ substantially in their cultural orientation, which has direct implications on how they are reached, in what language they can be effectively communicated, and what insights can be used to develop an effective marketing strategy.

CONCLUSIONS AND IMPLICATIONS

Moving forward, marketers who look to the Latino population for growth will need to continue to explore the nuances of the Latino consumer with greater precision. The rise and growth of the bicultural U.S.-born Latino will continue to pressure the marketing community to better discern and measure cultural differences within the Latino population, which a bidimensional cultural orientation scale can do quite effectively. Given that the future Latino demographic is projected to be increasingly bicultural and bilingual, the U.S. marketing community should be encouraged to place a greater effort on mastering the cultural levers of consumer behavior. My intention with this chapter is to not only spark discussions around a scale that measures cultural orientation among Latinos, but to propose the need to understand the changing Latino consumer bidimensionally and with greater cultural sensitivity.

Figure 2
A Nativity-Based View Conceptual Framework

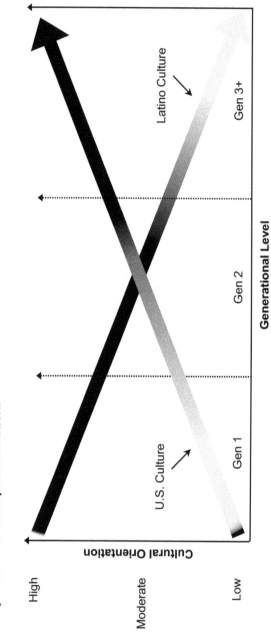

Source: The Center for Multicultural Science.

Table 2
U.S. Cultural Dimension Scores by Race and Nationality

	PDI	IDV	MAS	UAI	LTO	IVR
Non-Latino White	40	91	62	46	26	68
African American	34	89	65	34	37	80
Latino Mexican descent	35	85	69	45	35	83
Latino Puerto Rican descent	35	85	73	45	24	63
Latino Cuban descent	42	82	70	51	22	58
Chinese American	31	74	66	39	22	57

Note: PDI = Power Distance Index; IDV = Individualism-Collectivism, MAS = Masculinity, UAI = Uncertainty Avoidance Orientation, LTO = Long Term Orientation, IVR = Indulgence v. Restraint. Scores based on Hofstede's VSM 2013 formula.

Source: De Mooij, M. and Beniflah, J. (2016). Measuring Cross-Cultural Differences of Ethnic Groups Within Nations: Convergence or Divergence of Cultural Values? The Case of the United States. *Journal of International Consumer Marketing*. 29(1): 2-10.

Table 2.1
Cultural Dimension Scores by Country

	PDI	IDV	MAS	UAI	LTO	IVR
United States	40	91	62	46	26	68
Mexico	81	30	69	82	24	97
Costa Rica	38	15	21	86	n/a	n/a
Trinidad	47	16	58	56	13	80
Surinam	85	47	37	92	n/a	n/a
China	80	20	66	30	87	23
West Africa/Ghana	77	20	46	54	4	72
Puerto Rico	n/a	n/a	n/a	n/a	0	90

Note: PDI = Power Distance Index; IDV = Individualism-Collectivism, MAS = Masculinity, UAI = Uncertainty Avoidance Orientation, LTO = Long Term Orientation, IVR = Indulgence v. Restraint. Scores based on Hofstede's VSM 2013 formula.

Source: De Mooij, M. and Beniflah, J. (2016). Measuring Cross-Cultural Differences of Ethnic Groups Within Nations: Convergence or Divergence of Cultural Values? The Case of the United States. *Journal of International Consumer Marketing*. 29(1): 2-10.

Table 2.2
U.S. Cultural Dimension Scores by Nationality, Total and Nativity

	PDI	IDV	MAS	UAI	LTO	IVR
Mexican Total	35	85	69	45	35	83
Mexican U.S. Born	33	85	66	46	35	81
Mexican Foreign Born	40	86	73	41	36	86
U.S. Puerto Rican Total	35	85	73	45	24	63
Puerto Rican U.S. Born	33	84	71	41	24	65
Puerto Rican Foreign Born	44	90	83	63	24	51
Cuban Total	42	82	70	51	22	58
Cuban U.S. Born	50	80	73	50	25	63
Cuban Foreign Born	26	85	62	54	17	49
Chinese Total	31	74	66	39	22	57
Chinese U.S. Born	36	75	64	37	13	57
Chinese Foreign Born	18	68	75	44	48	58

Note: PDI = Power Distance Index; IDV = Individualism-Collectivism, MAS = Masculinity, UAI = Uncertainty Avoidance Orientation, LTO = Long Term Orientation, IVR = Indulgence v. Restraint. Scores based on Hofstede's VSM 2013 formula. Nativity is operationalized by U.S. born and foreign born.

Source: De Mooij, M. and Beniflah, J. (2016). Measuring Cross-Cultural Differences of Ethnic Groups Within Nations: Convergence or Divergence of Cultural Values? The Case of the United States. *Journal of International Consumer Marketing.* 29(1): 2-10.

Table 2.3
U.S. Cultural Dimension Scores by Race, Nationality, Total and Age

	PDI	IDV	MAS	UAI	LTO	IVR
Non-Latino White Total	40	91	62	46	26	68
Non-Latino White 18-34	42	89	67	49	29	65
Non-Latino White 35-49	39	93	57	44	23	71
Mexican Total	35	85	69	45	35	83
Mexican 18-34	30	81	69	44	30	88
Mexican 35-49	42	90	68	45	41	77
Cuban Total	42	82	70	51	22	58
Cuban 18-34	41	82	68	54	20	61
Cuban 35-49	42	81	72	47	26	54
Puerto Rican Total	35	85	73	45	24	68
Puerto Rican 18-34	43	89	75	36	35	61
Puerto Rican 35-49	26	80	71	55	13	65
African American Total	34	89	65	34	37	80
African American 18-34	35	95	69	41	47	75
African American 35-49	33	83	61	26	25	68
Chinese Total	31	74	66	39	22	57
Chinese 18-34	29	75	63	39	12	56
Chinese 35-49	34	72	71	38	33	59

Note: PDI = Power Distance Index; IDV = Individualism-Collectivism, MAS = Masculinity, UAI = Uncertainty Avoidance Orientation, LTO = Long Term Orientation, IVR = Indulgence v. Restraint. Scores based on Hofstede's VSM 2013 formula.

Source: De Mooij, M. and Beniflah, J. (2016). Measuring Cross-Cultural Differences of Ethnic Groups Within Nations: Convergenceor Divergence of Cultural Values? The Case of the United States. Journal of International Consumer Marketing. 29(1): 2-10.

Table 2.4
Cultural Orientation Mean Scores for U.S. Latinos by Generational Level

	Millennial	Generation X	Boomer
HCOS	3.5	3.7	3.5
ACOS	3.8	3.6	3.7

Source: Cortés-Vásquez, L., Montenegro, X., Willoth, S., Santiago, C., and Beniflah, J. (2014). Challenging the Belief that All U.S. Hispanics Are Culturally Homogeneous: An AHAA and AARP Cultural Orientation and Generational Study. *Journal of Brand Strategy.* 3(3): 235-244.

HCOS = Hispanic Cultural Orientation Scale. ACOS = Anglo Cultural Orientation Scale.

Table 2.5
Cultural Orientation Mean Scores for U.S. Latinos by Acculturation Level

	Low	Medium	High
HCOS	4.1	3.8	3.1
ACOS	3.2	4.0	4.2

Source: Cortés-Vásquez, L., Montenegro, X., Willoth, S., Santiago, C., and Beniflah, J. (2014). Challenging the Belief that All U.S. Hispanics Are Culturally Homogeneous: An AHAA and AARP Cultural Orientation and Generational Study. *Journal of Brand Strategy.* 3(3): 235-244.

HCOS = Hispanic Cultural Orientation Scale. ACOS = Anglo Cultural Orientation Scale.

Table 2.6
Cultural Orientation Mean Scores for Three U.S. Latino Generations by Nativity Level

	Millennial		Gen X		Boomer	
	Foreign Born	U.S. Born	Foreign Born	U.S. Born	Foreign Born	U.S. Born
HCOS	4.0	3.3	4.0	3.2	3.9	3.2
ACOS	3.5	4.1	3.3	4.1	3.4	4.1

Source: Cortés-Vásquez, L., Montenegro, X., Willoth, S., Santiago, C., and Beniflah, J. (2014). Challenging the Belief that All U.S. Hispanics Are Culturally Homogeneous: An AHAA and AARP Cultural Orientation and Generational Study. *Journal of Brand Strategy.* 3(3): 235-244.

HCOS = Hispanic Cultural Orientation Scale. ACOS = Anglo Cultural Orientation Scale.

CHAPTER TWO ENDNOTES

[24] Anderson, J. and Narus, J. (1998). Business Marketing: Understand What Customers Value. *Harvard Business Review.* November-December Issue. Accessed on January 10, 2020: https://hbr.org/1998/11/business-marketing-understand-what-customers-value.

[25] Beniflah, J., Chatterjee, S., and Curtis, K. (2014). Bilingual Memory: The Impact of Acculturation on the Cognitive Structure of Foreign-Born Hispanics. *Journal of Brand Strategy.* 3(3). Autumn/Fall (Multicultural Special Issue): 261-277.

[26] Boroditsky, L. (2011). How Language Shapes Thought. *Scientific American.* 302(2): 62-65.

[27] Chomsky, N. and Ronat, M. (2011). On Language. New York: New Press.

[28] Sapir, E. (1929). The Status of Linguistics as a Science. *Language.* 5: 207-214. Reprinted in the selected writings of Edward Sapir in Language, Culture, and Personality, ed. by D. G. Mandelbaum: 160-166. Berkeley: University of California Press.

[29] Whorf, B. (1940). Science and Linguistics. *Technology Review.* 42: 227-31, 247-8. Reprinted in Language, Thought, and Reality: Selected writings of Benjamin Lee Whorf, ed. by J. B. Carroll, 207-19. Cambridge, MA: The Technology Press of MIT/New York: Wiley. 1956.

[30] Marín, G. and Gamba, R. (1996). A New Measurement of Acculturation for Hispanics: The Bidimensional Acculturation Scale for Hispanics (BAS). *Hispanic Journal of Behavioral Sciences.* 18(3): 297-316.

[31] Ibid.

[32] Felix-Ortiz, M., Newcomb, M., and Myers, H. (1994). A Multidimensional Measure of Cultural Identity for Latino and Latina Adolescents. *Hispanic Journal of Behavioral Sciences.* 16(2): 99-115.

[33] Berry, J. and Sam, D. (1996). Acculturation and adaptation. In J. W. Berry. M. A. Segall and Kagitubasi (eds). *Handbook of Cross-Cultural Psychology: Social Behaviors and Application.* 3: 291-326. Boston: Allyn and Bacon.

[34] Beniflah, J., Chatterjee, S., and Curtis, K. (2014). Bilingual Memory: The Impact of Acculturation on the Cognitive Structure of Foreign-Born Hispanics. *Journal of Brand Strategy.* 3(3). Autumn/Fall (Multicultural Special Issue): 261-277.

[35] Cruz, T., Marshall, S., Bowling, J., *et al.* (2008). The Validity of a Proxy Acculturation Scale among U.S. Hispanics. *Hispanic Journal of Behavioral Sciences.* 30(4): 425-446.

[36] Marín, G. and Gamba, R. (1996). A New Measurement of Acculturation for Hispanics: The Bidimensional Acculturation Scale for Hispanics (BAS). *Hispanic Journal of Behavioral Sciences.* 18(3): 297-316.

[37] Cruz, T., Marshall, S., Bowling, J., *et al.* (2008). The Validity of a Proxy Acculturation Scale among U.S. Hispanics. *Hispanic Journal of Behavioral Sciences.* 30(4): 425-446.

[38] Szapocznik, J., Kurtines, W., and Fernandez, T. (1980). Bicultural Involvement and Adjustment in Hispanic-American Youths. *Intercultural Journal of Intercultural Relations.* (4)3-4: 353-65.

[39] Perez, W. and Padilla, A. (2000). Cultural Orientation Across Three Generations of Hispanic Adolescents. *Hispanic Journal of Behavioral Sciences.* 22(3): 390-398.

[40] Ibid.

[41] Ibid.

[42] Ibid.

[43] Krogstad, J., Stepler, R., and Lopez, M. (2015). English Proficiency on the Rise Among Latinos. Pew Research Center. Accessed on February 1, 2020: http://www.pewhispanic.org/2015/05/12/english-proficiency-on-the-rise-among-latinos/

[44] Beniflah, J., Hughes, B., and Garcia, C. (2015). Paradigm Shift: The Effect of Nativity and Years-In-Country on Television Program Viewing Across Three Hispanic Generational Levels. *Journal of Cultural Marketing Strategy.* 1(1): 19-31.

[45] De Mooij, M. and Beniflah, J. (2016). Measuring Cross-Cultural Differences of Ethnic Groups within Nations: Convergence or Divergence of Cultural Values? The Case of the United States. *Journal of International Consumer Marketing.* 29(1): 2-10.

[46] Ibid.

[47] Ibid.

[48] Coon, H. and Kemmelmeier, M. (2001). Cultural Orientations in the United States: (Re)examining Differences Among Ethnic Groups. *Journal of Cross-Cultural Psychology.* 32(1): 348-364.

[49] De Mooij, M. (2014). Global Marketing and Advertising. Understanding Cultural Paradoxes. Thousand Oaks: Sage.

[50] Hofstede, G. (2001). Culture's Consequences (2nd Ed.). Thousand Oaks: Sage.

[51] Hofstede, G., Hofstede, J., and Minkov, M. (2010a). Cultures and Organizations: Software of the Mind (3rd Ed.). New York: McGraw Hill.

[52] De Mooij, M. (2014). Global Marketing and Advertising. Understanding Cultural Paradoxes. Thousand Oaks: Sage.

[53] Hofstede, G., Hofstede, J., and Minkov, M. (2010a). Cultures and Organizations: Software of the Mind (3rd Ed.). New York: McGraw Hill.

[54] Ibid.

[55] Hofstede, G. (2001). Culture's Consequences (2nd Ed.). Thousand Oaks: Sage.

[56] De Mooij, M. (2015a). Cultural Marketing: Maximizing Business Effectiveness in a Multicultural World. *The Journal of Cultural Marketing Strategy.* 1(1): 11-18.

[57] Hofstede, G., Hofstede, J., and Minkov, M. (2010a). Cultures and Organizations: Software of the Mind (3rd Ed.). New York: McGraw Hill.

[58] Ibid.

[59] Ibid.

[60] Ibid.

[61] Ibid.

[62] Ibid.

[63] Ibid.

[64] De Mooij, M. and Beniflah, J. (2016). Measuring Cross-Cultural Differences of Ethnic Groups within Nations: Convergence or Divergence of Cultural Values? The Case of the United States. *Journal of International Consumer Marketing.* 29(1): 2-10.

[65] Ibid.

[66] Ibid.

[67] Coon, H. and Kemmelmeier, M. (2001). Cultural Orientations in the United States: (Re)examining Differences Among Ethnic Groups. *Journal of Cross-Cultural Psychology.* 32(1): 348-364.

[68] Gaines, S., Marelich, W., Bledsoe, K., *et al.* (1997). Links Between Race/Ethnicity and Cultural Values as Mediated by Racial/Ethnic Identity and Moderated by Gender. *Journal of Personality and Social Psychology.* 72(1): 1460-1476.

[69] De Mooij, M. and Beniflah, J. (2016). Measuring Cross-Cultural Differences of Ethnic Groups within Nations: Convergence or Divergence of Cultural Values? The Case of the United States. *Journal of International Consumer Marketing.* 29(1): 2-10.

[70] Ibid.

[71] Ibid.

[72] Ibid.

[73] Ibid.

[74] Ibid.

[75] Ibid.

[76] Ibid.

[77] Ibid.

[78] Ibid.

[79] Coon, H. and Kemmelmeier, M. (2001). Cultural Orientations in the United States: (Re)examining Differences Among Ethnic Groups. *Journal of Cross-Cultural Psychology*. 32(1): 348-364.

[80] Hofstede, G. (1980). Culture's Consequences. Beverly Hills: Sage.

[81] Hofstede, G., Garibaldi de Hilal, A., Malvezzi, S., *et al.* (2010b). Comparing Regional Cultures within a Country: Lessons from Brazil. *Journal of Cross-Cultural Psychology*. 41(1): 337-352.

[82] Mathur, A. (2012). Consumer Acculturation in the Age of Globalization: A Study of First-Generation Indian Immigrants in the United States. *Journal of International Consumer Marketing*. 24(1): 372-384.

[83] Patten, E. (2016). The Nation's Latino Population is Defined by its Youth: Nearly Half of U.S-Born Latinos are Younger than 18. The Pew Research Center. Accessed on January 23, 2020: http://www.pewhispanic. org/2016/04/20/the-nations-latino-population-is-defined-by-its-youth.

[84] Beniflah, J., Chatterjee, S., and Curtis, K. (2014). Bilingual Memory: The Impact of Acculturation on the Cognitive Structure of Foreign-Born Hispanics. *Journal of Brand Strategy*. 3(3). Autumn/Fall (Multicultural Special Issue): 261-277.

[85] Marín, G., Sabogal, F., Marín, B., *et al.* (1987). Development of a Short Acculturation Scale for Hispanics. *Hispanic Journal of Behavioral Sciences*. 9(2): 185-205.

[86] Szapocznik, J., Kurtines, W., and Fernandez, T. (1980). Bicultural Involvement and Adjustment in Hispanic-American Youths. *Intercultural Journal of Intercultural Relations*. 4(3-4): 353-365.

[87] Cortés-Vásquez, L., Montenegro, X., Willoth, S., Santiago, C., and Beniflah, J. (2014). Challenging the Belief that All U.S. Hispanics Are Culturally Homogeneous: An AHAA and AARP Cultural Orientation and Generational Study. *Journal of Brand Strategy*. 3(3): 235-244.

[88] Cruz, H., Marshall, S., Bowling, J., *et al.* (2008). The Validity of a Proxy Acculturation Scale Among U.S. Hispanics. *Hispanic Journal of Behavioral Sciences*. 30(4): 425-446.

[89] Ibid.

[90] Cortés-Vásquez, L., Montenegro, X., Willoth, S., Santiago, C., and Beniflah, J. (2014). Challenging the Belief that All U.S. Hispanics Are

Culturally Homogeneous: An AHAA and AARP Cultural Orientation and Generational Study. *Journal of Brand Strategy.* 3(3): 235-244.

[91] Szapocznik, J., Kurtines, W., and Fernandez, T. (1980). Bicultural Involvement and Adjustment in Hispanic-American Youths. *Intercultural Journal of Intercultural Relations.* 4(3–4): 353–365.

[92] Ibid.

[93] Cortés-Vásquez, L., Montenegro, X., Willoth, S., Santiago, C., and Beniflah, J. (2014). Challenging the Belief that All U.S. Hispanics Are Culturally Homogeneous: An AHAA and AARP Cultural Orientation and Generational Study. *Journal of Brand Strategy.* 3(3): 235-244.

[94] Ibid.

[95] Ibid.

[96] Ibid.

THREE

This chapter introduces the Nativity-Based View (NBV), a new approach that drives targeting effectiveness and media ROI with U.S. Latinos. This chapter draws from a linear acculturation model and deconstructs it. At its core, the NBV challenges the Hispanic Marketing Paradigm by segmenting the Latino population by nativity, generating key insights and driving advertising effectiveness. Our research has shown that nativity is a better predictor (than language) in understanding what Latinos consume in media,[97] which has significant media investment implications for brands. In this chapter, I provide an overview on: (1) the empirical framework on which the NBV is based; (2) the impact of nativity on demographics, language usage and (linear) television consumption by Latinos; and (3) the application of the NBV on media spend for three category-leading brands.

OVERVIEW

Significant shifts in the demographic landscape combined with the rise of digital media over the last 20 years have transformed the face of marketing in the United States. Yet, for more than three decades, marketing to U.S. Latinos has undergone little change with Spanish-language television continuing to represent the bulk of U.S. Latino media spend.[98] I propose that there is a better way to drive media ROI with the Latino population at a time when linear television viewership is slowly declining and digital and social media usage is almost ubiquitous among Latinos and other segments. This chapter advances the Nativity-Based View, a new way to plan and buy media for U.S. Latinos based on nativity. The results of a recent NBV study show that foreign-born and U.S.-born Latinos are not homogeneous in what they watch on linear television, suggesting that Spanish-language television is not the "best way" to reach all U.S. Latinos. When nativity is coupled with age, our research has found that approximately 80 percent of Spanish-language television does not reach Latino Millennials,[99] strongly suggesting that the NBV is a valuable tool in driving media ROI for brands.

The U.S. Latino population represents a significant marketing opportunity for major corporations. Latinos represent the largest ethnic group in the U.S. with almost 60 million in population[100] and a purchasing power in excess of $1.5 trillion.[101] By 2050, Latinos are projected to reach 100 million and account for an estimated 85 percent of the total U.S. population growth by 2050.[102] As such, it is not surprising that marketers in virtually every category consider Latinos an important growth segment. In addition, Spanish-language television has played a fundamental role in marketing to Latinos since the 1980s. In 2018, leading corporations spent an excess of $5 billion targeting Latinos on Spanish-language television, representing approximately 60 percent of total Spanish-language media spend.[103] To measure a growing Latino television audience, Nielsen introduced language quintiles in the early 1990s. This metric quantified language-use-at-home for U.S. Latinos across five levels: Quintile 1 measures

Latinos who speak "Spanish Only" at home; Quintile 2 measures Latinos who speak "More Spanish than English" at home; Quintile 3 measures Latinos who speak an "Equal amount of Spanish and English" at home; Quintile 4 measures Latinos who speak "More English than Spanish" at home; and Quintile 5 measures Latinos who speak "English Only" at home.

Nielsen's language quintiles are considered one of the most important measures in linear television viewing for Latinos and have helped make language "the" variable in Latino marketing. The demographic landscape, however, has evolved significantly since the 1980s, with Millennials and Gen Z adding almost 150 million new consumers in the U.S. over the last 20 years.[104] During this time, the media industry experienced a revolution of its own with digital surpassing linear television spend for the first time in 2016. Nevertheless, corporations continue to heavily invest in Spanish-language television as a way to reach U.S. Latinos. This is true despite the fact that the U.S. Latino population is hardly homogeneous: (a) 74 percent of Latinos (ages 34 and under) are U.S. born, while 61 percent of Latinos (Gen X and Boomers) are foreign born;[105] (b) Latinos are heavy users of digital and social media, as high as 85 percent are using their smartphones several times a day, and more Latinos across all ages use social media throughout the day;[106] and (c) Spanish-language proficiency varies significantly across all U.S. Latinos, thus making marketing to these consumers more nuanced and less straight-forward than in the past.[107]

Historically, one of the ways marketers have conceptualized the Latino population has been to report on the aggregate of this group and compare it with the non-Latino White population. This is considered a between-group research design. This chapter proposes a different approach. The NBV contends that a within-group design based on nativity can generate significant insights that drives media ROI for major corporations spending millions of dollars in Spanish-language television each year. Instead of using a language-based metric, the NBV offers a better way to target and measure the changing U.S. Latino television audience in the 21st century.

ACCULTURATION FRAMEWORKS

Acculturation is a complex process defined by the changes that groups or individuals undergo when they come into contact with a dominant culture.[108] Although there is general agreement that acculturation is an important topic of research, there is little agreement on how to conceptualize and measure it. Current theory suggests that acculturation is a multidimensional construct.[109] As such, researchers have proposed different scales to measure the degree to which an individual maintains their ethnic culture and the degree to which they participate in the host culture.[110] At least 20 acculturation scales have been used with the Latino population. These scales range in length from three to 69 items. The more widely used scales tend to be more comprehensive and therefore longer; for example, the Acculturation Rating Scale for Mexican Americans (ARSMA) consists of 20 items, and the revised bidimensional version, the ARSMA-II, contains 48 items in two separate scales, while the N-7, National Alcohol Survey (NAS) acculturation scale is a unidimensional scale based on 12 items.[111][112] Researchers who use large, routinely-collected data sets frequently rely on a single-proxy variable to represent acculturation. Typical examples of single proxy acculturation measures include place of birth, generational status, years (or proportion) of life lived in the U.S., language spoken at home and interview language. The most frequently used and strongest single indicator of acculturation is language use-at-home.[113] Generational status or nativity, and length of time residing in the U.S. are also standard markers of acculturation. The advantage of using these variables is that they are easy to assess, and they are regularly collected in large surveys. However, it is important to note that single-item proxies of acculturation have been found to have low validity and reliability and should be used mindfully.[114]

As shown in Figure 3, the empirical framework for NBV is based on the deconstruction of a popular linear acculturation scale comprised of four variables. The four-item Proxy Acculturation Scale (PAS-4) incorporates two language items (language-use-at-home and the language of the survey) and two markers of exposure to the U.S. (generational status and proportion of life lived in the U.S.). The PAS-4 has high internal consistency, has a high correlation to the NAS, provides a more sensitive measure of acculturation than the proxy variables taken individually, and has similar correlations among subpopulations by country of ancestry.[115]

The NBV framework deconstructs the popular PAS-4 and examines the effect of nativity on three dependent variables (demographics, language-use-at-home, and television viewership). The NBV has significant implications. First, it challenges the Hispanic Marketing Paradigm. Secondly, the NBV is an innovative media approach, which can serve as an alternative to an outdated, demographic-based model that media buyers and planners have been using for decades. Thirdly, the NBV has been shown to drive targeting effectiveness and media ROI with U.S. Latinos, saving corporations millions, sometimes tens of millions, of dollars. In this chapter, I argue that measuring U.S. Latinos in aggregate is an oversimplification. As corporations seek to maximize sales and drive ROI, I contend that the use of nativity provides marketers with greater nuances in understanding this diverse population and an improved media ROI.

THE IMPACT OF NATIVITY ON DEMOGRAPHICS

Not only are Latinos changing the overall demographic composition of the total U.S. population, but the Latino population itself is undergoing unprecedented change. Between 1980 and 2000, immigration was the main driver of Latino population growth, as Latino immigrants boomed from 4.2 million to 14.1 million.[116] Since 2000, however, the primary source of Latino population growth has swung from immigration to native births.[117] Between 2000 and 2010, there were 9.6 million Latino births in the U.S., while the number of newly arrived immigrants was 6.5 million.[118] Overall, U.S. births alone accounted for 60 percent of Latino population growth, and will continue to drive growth for this ethnic group well into the 21st century.[119] The rise of U.S. born and the slowdown of foreign-born Latino population growth have begun to reshape the adult Latino population. With the slowdown of immigration, the number of U.S.-born Latinos entering adulthood is beginning to accelerate. Today, some 800,000 young U.S.-born Latinos enter adulthood each year; however, in the coming decades that number will rise to more than a million annually. Even as the share of Latino immigrants decreases, rapid growth in the number of Latino births means that the Latino population will continue to grow at a steady rate. Latinos are the nation's largest ethnic group and one of the fastest growing. Since 1970, the Latino population has increased six-fold, from 9.1 million to 53 million in 2012.[120] According to the latest figures from the U.S. Census Bureau, U.S. Latinos are projected to grow to 129 million by 2060.[121] Its share of the U.S. population, currently at 18 percent, is expected to reach 31 percent by 2060.[122]

In fact, as shown in Table 3, 74 percent of U.S.-born Latinos are Millennial and younger (ages 34 and under), 14 percent are Generation X (ages 35-49), 9 percent are Boomers (ages 50–68), and 3 percent are from the Silent Generation (ages 69 and older).[123] On the other hand, 32 percent of foreign-born Latinos are Millennial and younger (ages 34 and under), 37 percent belong to Generation X (ages 35-49), 24 percent are Boomers (ages 50-68), and 7 percent are from the Silent Generation (ages 69 and older).[124] This data suggests that U.S.-born Latinos are younger in age, while foreign-born Latinos are older (61 percent are Generation X and Boomers). These age differences by nativity (U.S. born and foreign born) are significant and have major implications on marketing to Latinos.

THE IMPACT OF NATIVITY ON LANGUAGE

This section examines the relationship between nativity and language-use-at-home for U.S. Latinos. The data challenge the popular notion that Spanish is the preferred language for all U.S. Latinos. Assessing language-use-at-home by quintile, recent research has found that in aggregate, the data is evenly distributed across the five levels.[125] When examining the effect of nativity on language-use-at-home, however, significant differences were found: Among first-generation Latinos, 61.2 percent spoke "Spanish Only" and "More Spanish than English."[126] Among second-generation Latinos, 60.9 percent spoke "English Only" and "More English than Spanish."[127] For third-generation Latinos, 90.5 percent spoke "English Only" and "More English than Spanish" (see Table 3.1).[128]

The Pew Hispanic Center uses a measure known as primary

language which combines survey respondent self-assessments of English and Spanish speaking and reading ability into a single measure of language ability. It is meant to summarize speaking and reading ability in both English and Spanish. Using the self-reported measures of English and Spanish proficiency in speaking and reading, survey respondents are classified in three ways: Spanish-dominant, bilingual and English-dominant. Respondents are classified as Spanish-dominant if they say they speak and read Spanish very well or pretty well, but their ratings of English ability in the same two categories are lower. Respondents are considered English-dominant if they say they are more proficient in English than in Spanish. Finally, bilingual respondents are those who say they are proficient in both English and Spanish. Using this measure, the survey found that 38 percent of Latino adults are Spanish-dominant, another 38 percent are bilingual and the remainder (24 percent) are English-dominant.[129]

Understanding which language is more dominant is a function of a number of factors, including generational level or nativity, years-in-country, and others. Among foreign-born Latinos (first-generation), the majority (61 percent) are Spanish-dominant, one-third (33 percent) are bilingual, and just 6 percent are English-dominant.[130] Among second-generation Latinos, Spanish dominance falls to 8 percent, but the share of bilingual Latinos rises to 53 percent, and the English-dominant share increases to 40 percent.[131] By the third generation, almost all Latinos are either bilingual (29 percent) or English-dominant (69 percent).[132]

THE IMPACT OF NATIVITY ON TELEVISION VIEWING

This section examines the relationship between nativity and television viewing among U.S. Latinos. The data challenge the popular notion that Spanish-language television is the "best way" to target U.S. Latinos. According to the Pew Hispanic Center, among U.S. Latinos, more watch English-language television than Spanish language programs (45 percent versus 28 percent).[133] Meanwhile, 26 percent report using both languages equally.[134] Across three generational levels, conversely, the consumption of English-language television increases, while Spanish-language television decreases.[135] Among foreign-born Latinos, nearly twice as many say they watch Spanish-language television compared to English (40 percent versus 25 percent).[136] One-third (34 percent) report watching television in English and Spanish Equally.[137] By the second-generation, 69 percent of Latinos say they watch television in Mostly or Only in English, 17 percent report watching television in English and Spanish Equally, and 12 percent report watching television Mostly or Only in Spanish.[138] Among third-generation Latinos, 83 percent report watching television in English; 11 percent report watching television in both languages, and just 5 percent of third-generation Latinos report watching television Mostly or Only in Spanish.[139]

A 2019 ThinkNow study reports that U.S.-born Latinos watch television that skews toward English – with 81 percent saying they prefer to watch television in Only English, 10 percent Mostly in English but Some Spanish, 8 percent Mostly in Spanish but Some English, and just 1 percent in Only Spanish. Meanwhile, 14 percent of foreign-born Latinos report a preference for watching television in Only English, 26 percent Mostly in English but Some Spanish, 27 percent Mostly in Spanish but Some English, and

22 percent in Only Spanish. These data suggest that there is no single television viewership pattern across all Latinos.

A 2016 survey-based study published in the *Journal of Cultural Marketing Strategy* found that Univision was said to be the most watched television network among first-generation Latinos, and the fifth most watched television network among second-generation Latinos across all dayparts (see Table 3.2).[140] Among third-generation television, Univision was the seventh most watched network.[141] Two interesting patterns emerged: (1) as generational levels increased, Spanish-language television network viewing among U.S. Latinos decreased; and (2) as generational levels increased, English-language television network viewing increased.[142] These findings challenge the popular notion that Spanish-language television is the "best way" to reach Latinos, and suggest that marketers should consider alternative media publishers to reach different segments of the U.S. Latino population.

We also examined C3 television viewership data for U.S. Latinos during primetime in 2015 for two demographic segments, 18-34 and 35-49. The findings were surprising: seven of the top ten television networks during primetime for foreign-born Latinos (18-34 and 35-49) were in Spanish (see Table 3.3).[143] Conversely, C3 television viewership data for U.S.-born Latinos showed that eight of the top ten television networks during primetime were in English.[144] The two Spanish-language networks to rank in the top ten television networks watched by U.S.-born Latinos were Univision and Telemundo.[145] Among U.S.-born Latinos (18-34), Univision and Telemundo ranked first and fourth, respectively, while among the older age demographic (35-49), Univision ranked fifth and Telemundo ranked sixth (see Table 3.4).[146] Not surprisingly, U.S.-born Latinos show a preference for English-language television over Spanish-language television. These findings have significant investment implications for marketers and challenge the 30-year-old marketing tenet that Spanish-language television is the "best way" to reach U.S. Latinos.

A 2018 analysis of C3 television viewership data during primetime for 18-34 and 35-49 U.S. Latinos were consistent with our past research: Six of the top ten television networks during primetime for foreign-born Latinos (18-34 and 35-49) were in Spanish (see Table 3.5).[147] The top three television networks for foreign-born Latinos (18-34) were Univision, Telemundo and UniMás, respectively.[148] The ratings were higher for the older Latino cohort (35-49) across these three in-language networks.[149] Conversely, U.S.-born Latinos show a preference for English-language television, regardless of age. Seven and eight of the top ten television networks during primetime for U.S.-born Latinos (18-34 and 35-49), respectively, were in English (see Table 3.6).[150] The top three television networks for U.S.-born Latinos (18-34) were Univision, Telemundo and ABC, respectively. For U.S.-born Latinos (35-49), the top three television networks were NBC, ABC and FOX, respectively.[151]

As shown in Table 3.7, a more recent analysis of C3 television viewership data among Latino 18+ in the first quarter of 2020 reveal an all too familiar pattern. Six of the top ten television networks in 2020 for foreign-born Latinos (18+) were in Spanish: Univision (#1), Telemundo (#2), UniMás (#3), Estrella (#4), Galavision (#5), and Discovery in Español (#7).[152] On the other hand, for the U.S.-born Latino (18+), eight of the top 10 networks were in English, with Univision ranking third and Telemundo ranking sixth.[153] Data shows that no matter the timeframe (i.e., year or quarter) or age, foreign-born Latinos prefer Spanish-language linear television, while U.S.-born Latinos show just the opposite pattern. What does change is the ranking of the networks.

THE IMPACT OF NATIVITY ON MEDIA ROI

Three tests were additionally conducted using 2019 competitive television spend and C3 television viewership data, both measured by Nielsen. Three leading brands today were examined across different categories (QSR, automotive, and wireless). Given that brands consider Millennials an important growth segment, our study measured the effectiveness in reaching Latino Millennials with Spanish-language television. The results were surprising.

As shown in Table 3.8, a leading wireless brand spent an estimated $39 million in 2019 on Spanish-language television.[154] The NBV analysis showed that $7.5 million (19 percent of the total budget) reached Latino Millennials (18-34); $11.2 million (29 percent) to Latinos, ages 35-49; and $20.3 million (52 percent of the total budget) to Latinos, ages 50 and over.[155] Most surprisingly, the NBV analysis revealed that approximately 19 percent of this advertiser's budget reached Latino Millennials compared to 81 percent to Latinos, ages 35 and above.[156] Additionally, this leading wireless brand spent approximately $33.4 million (86 percent) of its total budget reaching foreign-born Latinos and $5.6 million (14 percent) to U.S.-born Latinos.[157]

As shown in Table 3.9, the NBV analysis was conducted for a leading brand in the automotive category. Out of an estimated $62.6 million spent in 2019 on Spanish-language television, $12.1 million (19 percent) reached Latino Millennials (18-34); $18 million (29 percent) to Latinos, ages 35-49; and $32.5 million (52 percent of the total budget) to Latinos, ages 50 and over.[158] Interestingly, the NBV analysis revealed that approximately 19 percent of this advertiser's budget reached Latino Millennials compared to 81 percent to Latinos, ages 35 and above.[159] Additionally, this leading automotive brand spent approximately

$53.6 million (86 percent) of its total budget reaching foreign-born Latinos and $9 million (14 percent) to U.S.-born Latinos.

Lastly, Table 3.10 shows the NBV analysis for a leading brand in the QSR category. Out of an estimated $69 million spent in 2019 on Spanish-language television, $13.3 million (19 percent) reached Latino Millennials (18-34); $19.8 million (29 percent) to Latinos, ages 35-49; and $35.9 million (52 percent) to Latinos, ages 50 and over.[160] Interestingly, the NBV revealed that approximately 19 percent of this advertiser›s budget reached Latino Millennials with 81 percent to Latinos, ages 35 and above.[161] Additionally, this leading QSR brand spent approximately $59.2 million (86 percent) reaching foreign-born Latinos and $9.8 million (14 percent) to U.S.-born Latinos.[162]

CONCLUSIONS AND IMPLICATIONS

This chapter challenges a central tenet that has driven Latino marketing for more than 30 years, namely that Spanish-language television is the single "best way" to reach all U.S Latinos. The debate is not whether or not to invest in linear television or digital. Or in the Latino consumer. The question should be: how much should brands invest in linear television, digital and other forms of media (regardless of language) to reach their intended Latino target? This chapter has shown that (1) foreign-born Latinos prefer Spanish-language linear television programming compared to U.S.-born Latinos; (2) U.S.-born Latinos prefer English-language linear television programming compared to foreign-born Latinos; and (3) when nativity is coupled with age, a nuanced measure is created that quantifies the audience reach of Spanish-language television programming and how much is allocated by age and nativity. This new measure is incredibly useful for agencies and brands interested in driving media ROI.

The Nativity-Based View provides significant benefit to media planning and buying for Latinos in virtually every business sector. Advertising agencies can use the NBV as a media tool to help measure television audience and drive media return-on-investment. Needless to say, this level of granularity can improve key investment decisions for brands. In 2019, corporations reportedly spent more than $6 billion in Spanish-language television[163] and the NBV can help agencies target their core Latino segments with greater precision. For example, if brands are interested in targeting Latino Millennials effectively, the NBV can help quantify how much should be spent against this specific demographic. This type of precision based on nativity had an immediate impact in the 2016-17 Upfront season during which MAGNA announced the re-allocation of $250 million from linear television to digital.[164] Since then, the NBV has been responsible for an additional shift of $200 million to digital from linear television.[165] The adoption of the NBV in television planning and buying can improve media ROI significantly for brands. The NBV has also been utilized to analyze the reach of other ethnic consumers across other media, including digital and linear radio. As multicultural consumers make up the majority of the mainstream, more companies will continue to use the NBV and other models to help drive media ROI in a diverse America.

Figure 3
The Acculturation-Based Empirical Framework

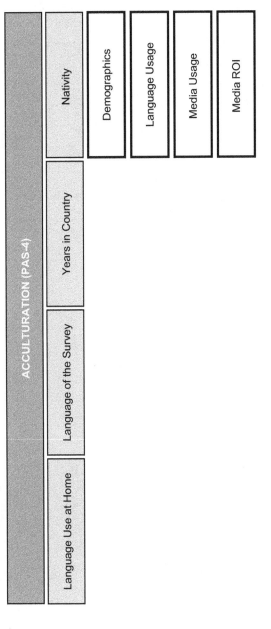

Source: Beniflah, J. and Hughes, B. (2016). An Industry Response: There *is* a Better Way to Target the U.S. Hispanic Television Audience. *Journal of Cultural Marketing Strategy.* 1(2): 170-179.

Table 3
Latino Population Across Five Generations by Nativity Level

	Foreign Born	U.S. Born
17 and Under	6%	47%
Gen Y	26%	27%
Gen X	37%	14%
Boomer	24%	9%
Silent Generation	7%	3%
Total	100%	100%

Source: Patten, E. (2016). The Nation's Latino Population is Defined by Its Youth: Nearly Half of U.S.-born Latinos Are Younger Than 18. The Pew Research Center. Accessed on January 23, 2020: http://www.pewhispanic.org/2016/04/20/the-nations-latino-population-is-defined-by-its-youth.

Table 3.1
Language Quintiles for U.S. Latinos by Nativity Level and Total

Language Use at Home	Gen 1	Gen 2	Gen 3+	Total
Spanish Only	26.5%	3.9%	0.3%	14.3%
More Spanish than English	34.7%	9.7%	0.3%	19.9%
About the Same	23.8%	25.5%	8.9%	20.6%
More English than Spanish	10.3%	37.4%	29.2%	21.9%
English Only	4.7%	23.5%	61.3%	23.3%
Total	100%	100%	100%	100%

Source: Beniflah, J., Hughes, B. and Garcia, C. (2015). Paradigm Shift: The Effect of Nativity and Years-in-Country on Television Program Viewing across Three Hispanic Generational Levels. *Journal of Cultural Marketing Strategy.* 1(1): 19-31.

Table 3.2
Television Networks Watched by U.S. Latinos by Nativity Level

Network	Gen 1	Gen 2	Gen 3+
ABC	28.9%	62.6%	60.1%
Azteca America	25.2%	5.2%	1.4%
CBS	25.1%	41.6%	62.4%
CW	9.1%	19.1%	21.1%
Estrella	16.1%	4.2%	1.1%
FOX	31.6%	54.8%	53.8%
MundoFOX	20.9%	4.2%	1.4%
NBC	24.6%	46.8%	52.4%
Telemundo	58.1%	18.1%	5.5%
UniMás	31.4%	8.4%	1.7%
Univision	63.8%	25.8%	6.2%
Other	8.3%	7.4%	8.3%
None of the Above	3.3%	8.4%	6.6%
Do Not Watch Broadcast TV	4.5%	9.1%	14.1%

Source: Beniflah, J., Hughes, B. and Garcia, C. (2015). Paradigm Shift: The Effect of Nativity and Years-in-Country on Television Program Viewing across Three Hispanic Generational Levels. *Journal of Cultural Marketing Strategy.* 1(1): 19-31.

Table 3.3
Q1 2015 Ratings-Based Ranking of TV Networks in Primetime for Foreign-Born Latinos by Age

Ranking (18-34)	Network	Ranking (35-49)	Network
1	Univision	1	Univision
2	Telemundo	2	Telemundo
3	UniMás	3	UniMás
4	Disc en español	4	Estrella
5	NBC	5	NBC
6	Galavision	6	MundoFOX
7	Estrella	7	Disc en español
8	FOX	8	ABC
9	ABC	9	Galavision
10	Azteca America	10	FOX

Source: Nielsen C3 TV ratings, Q1 2015. Copyrighted information ©2015 of The Nielsen Company, licensed for use herein.

Table 3.4
Q1 2015 Ratings-Based Ranking of TV Networks in Primetime for U.S.-Born Latinos by Age

Ranking (18-34)	Network	Ranking (35-49)	Network
1	Univision	1	NBC
2	FOX	2	FOX
3	NBC	3	CBS
4	Telemundo	4	ABC
5	ABC	5	Univision
6	CBS	6	Telemundo
7	CW	7	AMC
8	Adult Swim	8	CW
9	TBS	9	ESPN
10	ABC Family	10	USA Network

Source: Nielsen C3 TV ratings, Q1 2015. Copyrighted information ©2015 of The Nielsen Company, licensed for use herein.

Table 3.5
Q1 2018 Ratings-Based Ranking of TV Networks in Primetime for Foreign-Born Latinos by Age

Ranking (18-34)	Network	Ranking (35-49)	Network
1	Univision	1	Univision
2	Telemundo	2	Telemundo
3	UniMás	3	UniMás
4	Galavision	4	Estrella
5	Uni Deportes	5	Uni Deportes
6	Estrella	6	Galavision
7	Adult Swim	7	NBC
8	FOX	8	FOX
9	NBC	9	ABC
10	ABC	10	CBS

Source: Nielsen C3 TV ratings, Q1 2018. Copyrighted information ©2018 of The Nielsen Company, licensed for use herein.

Table 3.6
**Q1 2018 Ratings-Based Ranking of TV Networks in Primetime
for U.S.-Born Latinos by Age**

Ranking (18-34)	Network	Ranking (35-49)	Network
1	Univision	1	NBC
2	Telemundo	2	ABC
3	ABC	3	FOX
4	Adult Swim	4	CBS
5	Uni Deportes	5	Telemundo
6	NBC	6	Univision
7	TNT	7	CW
8	USA	8	USA
9	ESPN	9	TBS
10	CW	10	ESPN

Source: Nielsen C3 TV ratings, Q1 2018. Copyrighted information ©2018 of The
Nielsen Company, licensed for use herein.

Table 3.7
**Q1 2020 Ratings-Based Ranking of TV Networks for U.S. Latinos (18+)
by Nativity Level**

Ranking (Foreign Born)	Network	Ranking (U.S. Born)	Network
1	Univision	1	NBC
2	Telemundo	2	FOX
3	UniMás	3	Univision
4	Estrella	4	ABC
5	Galavision	5	CBS
6	NBC	6	Telemundo
7	Disc en español	7	CW
8	FOX	8	USA
9	ABC	9	MTV
10	CBS	10	TBS

Source: Nielsen C3 TV ratings, Q1 2020. Copyrighted information ©2020 of The Nielsen Company, licensed for use herein.

Table 3.8
NBV Analysis for Leading Wireless Brand in 2019 By Age, Nativity and Total

	18-34	35-49	50+	Total
Estimated Spend (Foreign Born)	$5.1	$10.1	$18.3	$33.4
% Spend (Foreign Born)	13%	26%	47%	86%
Estimated Spend (U.S. Born)	$2.4	$1.6	$2.0	$5.6
% Spend (U.S. Born)	6%	11.2%	20.3%	14%
Total Spend	$7.5	$11.2	$20.3	$39.0
% of Total Spend by Age	19%	29%	52%	100%

Source: Nielsen 2019 competitive spend and Spanish-language TV C3 data. NBV analysis conducted by MAGNA and the Center for Multicultural Science. Copyrighted information ©2019 of The Nielsen Company, licensed for use herein.

Table 3.9
NBV Analysis for Leading Automotive Brand in 2019 By Age, Nativity and Total

	18-34	35-49	50+	Total
Estimated Spend (Foreign Born)	$8.2	$16.1	$29.3	$53.6
% Spend (Foreign Born)	13%	26%	47%	86%
Estimated Spend (U.S. Born)	$3.9	$1.9	$3.2	$9.0
% Spend (U.S. Born)	6%	3%	5%	14%
Total Spend	12.1%	$18.0	$32.5	$62.6
% of Total Spend by Age	19%	29%	52%	100%

Source: Nielsen 2019 competitive spend and Spanish-language TV C3 data. NBV analysis conducted by MAGNA and the Center for Multicultural Science. Copyrighted information ©2019 of The Nielsen Company, licensed for use herein.

Table 3.10
NBV Analysis for Leading QSR Brand in 2019 By Age, Nativity and Total

	18-34	35-49	50+	Total
Estimated Spend (Foreign Born)	$9.0	$17.8	$32.4	$59.2
% Spend (Foreign Born)	13%	26%	47%	86%
Estimated Spend (U.S. Born)	$4.3	$2.0	$3.5	$9.8
% Spend (U.S. Born)	6%	3%	5%	14%
Total Spend	$13.3	19.8	$35.9	$69.0
% of Total Spend by Age	19%	29%	52%	100%

Source: Nielsen 2019 competitive spend and Spanish-language TV C3 data. NBV analysis conducted by MAGNA and the Center for Multicultural Science. Copyrighted information ©2019 of The Nielsen Company, licensed for use herein.

CHAPTER THREE ENDNOTES

[97] Beniflah, J. and Hughes, B. (2016). An Industry Response: There *is* a Better Way to Target the U.S. Hispanic Television Audience. *Journal of Cultural Marketing Strategy.* 1(2): 170-179.

[98] Hispanic Fact Pack. (2019). *AdAge.* New York: Crain Communications, Inc.

[99] Beniflah, J. (2019). The Nativity-Based View Media Usage and Allocation Study: Part 2. Unpublished Study.

[100] U.S. Census Bureau, 2019.

[101] Humphreys, J. (2018) The Multicultural Economy Report. Selig Center for Economic Growth, Terry College of Business, The University of Georgia. Atlanta, Georgia.

[102] U.S. Census Bureau, Population Projections.

[103] Hispanic Fact Pack. (2019). *AdAge.* New York: Crain Communications, Inc.

[104] U.S. Census Bureau, 2019.

[105] Patten, E. (2016). The Nation's Latino Population is defined by its youth: nearly half of U.S.-born Latinos are younger than 18. The Pew Research Center. Accessed on January 23, 2020: http://www.pewhispanic. org/2016/04/20/the-nations-latino-population-is-defined-by-its-youth

[106] ThinkNow, 2020.

[107] Ibid.

[108] Berry, J., Phinney, J., Sam, D. L., *et al.* (Eds.) (2006). Immigrant Youth in Cultural Transition: Acculturation Identity and Adaptation Across National Boundaries. London: Lawrence Erlbaum.

[109] Marín, G. and Gamba, R. (1996). A New Measurement of Acculturation for Hispanics: The Bidimensional Acculturation Scale for Hispanics (BAS). *Hispanic Journal of Behavioral Sciences.* 18(3): 297-316.

[110] Ibid.

[111] Cuéllar, I., Arnold, B., and Maldonado, R. (1995). Acculturation Rating Scale for Mexican Americans – II: A Revision of the Original ARSMA Scale. Hispanic *Journal of Behavioral Sciences.* 17(3): 275–304.

[112] Cruz, T., Marshall, S., Bowling, J. *et al.* (2008). The Validity of a Proxy Acculturation Scale Among U.S. Hispanics. *Hispanic Journal of Behavioral Sciences.* 30(4): 425-446.

[113] Ibid.

[114] Ibid.

[115] Ibid.

[116] U.S. Census Bureau, 2020.

[117] Ibid.

[118] Ibid.

[119] Ibid.

[120] Ibid.

[121] Ibid.

[122] Ibid.

[123] Patten, E. (2016). The Nation's Latino Population is Defined by its Youth: Nearly Half of U.S.-Born Latinos are Younger than 18. The Pew Research Center. Accessed on January 23, 2020: http://www.pewhispanic.org/2016/04/20/the-nations-latino-population-is-defined-by-its-youth

[124] Ibid.

[125] ThinkNow, 2020.

[126] Beniflah, J., Hughes, B., and Garcia, C. (2015). Paradigm Shift: The Effect of Nativity and Years-in-Country on Television Program Viewing across Three Hispanic Generational Levels. *Journal of Cultural Marketing Strategy*. 1(1): 19-31.

[127] Ibid.

[128] Ibid.

[129] Taylor, P., Lopez, M., Martínez, J., and Velasco, G. (2012). When Labels Don't Fit: Hispanics and their Views of Identity. Accessed on July 2, 2020: https://www.pewresearch.org/hispanic/2012/04/04/iv-language-use-among-latinos/

[130] Ibid.

[131] Ibid.

[132] Ibid.

[133] Ibid.

[134] Ibid.

[135] Ibid.

[136] Ibid.

[137] Ibid.

[138] Ibid.

[139] Ibid.

[140] Beniflah, J. and Hughes, B. (2016). An Industry Response: There *is* a Better Way to Target the U.S. Hispanic Television Audience. *Journal of Cultural Marketing Strategy*. 1(2): 170-179.

[141] Ibid.

[142] Ibid.

[143] Beniflah, J., Hughes, B., and Carrasco, M. (2018). Nativity-Based View: A New Audience Measurement Standard That Drives Television

Return-On-Investment for U.S. Hispanics. *Journal of Cultural Marketing Strategy.* 3(2): 43-59.

[144] Ibid.

[145] Ibid.

[146] Ibid.

[147] Ibid.

[148] Ibid.

[149] Ibid.

[150] Ibid.

[151] Ibid.

[152] Ibid.

[153] Ibid.

[154] Ibid.

[155] Ibid.

[156] Ibid.

[157] Ibid.

[158] Ibid.

[159] Ibid.

[160] Ibid.

[161] Ibid.

[162] Ibid.

[163] Hispanic Fact Pack. (2019). *AdAge.* New York: Crain Communications, Inc.

[164] Vranica, S. (2014). Interpublic to Shift $250 Million in TV Ad Spending to YouTube. *The Wall Street Journal.* Accessed on August 1, 2020: https://www.wsj.com/articles/interpublic-to-shift-250-million-in-tv-ad-spending-to-youtube-1462359623

[165] The Center for Multicultural Science estimates, 2020.

CHAPTER
FOUR

"If you're not doing multicultural marketing, you're not doing marketing." This notable phrase has been attributed to Marc Pritchard, Chief Brand Officer of Procter & Gamble, when he delivered a powerful keynote speech at the Cannes Lions Festival in 2018.[166] It captured the attention of almost every marketer in the advertising industry because it was the first time a major advertiser had underscored the importance of the multicultural population as a part of mainstream marketing. The U.S. Census has projected that the multicultural population will make up a numerical majority by 2043,[167] so few can disagree with Mr. Pritchard. The question that continues to loom over the advertising and marketing industry, however, is how does corporate America adapt to a changing marketplace?

In this chapter, I revisit in-culture marketing, a model that has served as the strategic backbone to the Hispanic Marketing Paradigm for more than three decades. I also take on the misguided "total market" approach used by leading general market ad agencies. Instead, I propose rightsizing the cultural silo and placing multicultural consumers front and center of mainstream marketing. This is truly revolutionary, if not paradigm shifting. It will not be easy. But these changes will help all brands increase growth and marketing effectiveness in an increasingly diverse America.

This chapter introduces two theories in social psychology that can help brands understand how to market to a multicultural population: (1) Self-Referencing,[168] which has shown to drive advertising effectiveness when information is linked to the self,[169] [170] and (2) Optimal Distinctiveness Theory,[171][172] which helps explain social identity and how people come to define themselves in terms of their social group memberships. The chapter concludes by advancing an empirical model that synthesizes this research. These theories will help brands develop strategically sound, self-referencing content to their diverse customer base, while reducing any concerns of alienating other important segments of the population.

IN-CULTURE MARKETING

In-culture marketing needs to be revisited. This does not mean that culture is not important in connecting with today's consumer, nor does it mean that those in charge of ethnic marketing are not important. Just the contrary. We must reassess, however, what in-culture marketing means in a multicultural America. It no longer makes sense to place Latino marketing in a silo, characterize U.S. Latinos by language, and define mainstream marketing by non-Latino White consumers. Instead, I propose a bold vision: Marketing in the 21st century will be characterized by a multicultural mainstream, which will transform marketing as we know it. The traditional ethnic and racial silo that was once created specifically for minority populations will rightsize commensurately. Marketing strategy (i.e., consumer insights, etc.) will be powered by Brown and Black across all business categories. It is a matter of when, not if.

Let me explain why it is important that we question the usefulness of in-culture marketing moving forward. Historically, ethnic marketing started as a silo and in-culture marketing served as its underlying methodology. Today, the majority of the population in the nation's largest cities is currently a multicultural majority, with Latinos driving population growth faster than any other group. Different times call for different measures.

The notion that Latinos prefer to speak Spanish at home and have their advertising in-language is at the center of the Hispanic Marketing Paradigm. Understandably, this has seldomly been questioned, given its importance to the advertising and marketing business. Latinos may prefer Spanish-language content compared to their non-Latino counterparts, but there is no scientific study to date that shows that *all* Latinos prefer speaking Spanish or prefer advertising in Spanish over English.[173] Much of our Nativity-Based View research challenges the homogeneous view of U.S. Latinos.

Moving forward, the U.S. advertising and marketing industry will need to agree on the nomenclature used to describe marketing in the 21st century. In this book, I have put forth the notion that marketing in a multicultural America is inherently multicultural, cross-cultural or cultural in nature. As a result, I see the changing demography blurring the lines between ethnic and general market ad agencies to the point where they will converge on each other's capabilities. General market agencies will be responsible for siloed marketing while traditional ethnic agencies will drive mainstream marketing. The structure of the industry will slowly converge, and advertising agencies will expand their capabilities in reaching and engaging with new consumer segments. The traditional in-language silo will continue to focus on the needs of the specific segments of the population that cannot be reached by mainstream marketing. The ethnic consumer, which has been conveniently siloed for decades, will define the New Mainstream.

MODELS OF TARGETING EFFECTIVENESS

As I said before, in-culture marketing is a conceptual model that has played a significant role in building and sustaining Latino marketing in the United States for more than 30 years. I strongly believe in the value of culture, and in leveraging this construct in a multicultural America. The principles of marketing will not change in an increasingly diverse America; what will change is the practice of marketing. The New Mainstream is Black and Brown and more diverse than ever. Corporate America will need to understand these consumers better because they are no longer a minority. They represent the majority of consumers who are also likely to be their core customers. In this section, I introduce two frameworks rooted in social psychology — Self-Referencing and Optimal Distinctiveness Theory — that can help marketers apply the marketing concept in the New Mainstream.[174]

SELF-REFERENCING

In cognitive psychology, self-referencing is defined as the cognitive processes individuals use to understand incoming information that pertains to them by comparing it to self-relevant information stored in memory.[175] Studies in psychology have demonstrated that self-referencing enhances learning and recall of information.[176] [177] The main explanation for these findings is that self-referencing facilitates elaboration of incoming information because the self is a highly organized, complex memory structure.[178] [179]

In consumer research, self-referencing has been found to affect persuasion.[180-182] The research has also identified some of the conditions when self-referencing enhances persuasion. For instance, studies find that self-referencing increases product feature and ad message elaboration and recall, but only enhances persuasion when message arguments or product features are strong, not weak.[183] These results support the theory that self-referencing facilitates elaboration of incoming information; when the information is related to the self-concept, elaboration is increased and strong arguments are favored over weak arguments.

Other researchers have found that self-referencing enhances persuasion to a certain point.[184] [185] That is, moderate levels of self-referencing enhance persuasion, while high levels of self-referencing actually reduce persuasion. Similar to the Resource Matching Hypothesis,[186] too much self-referencing, like too much elaboration, leads to unrelated thought processes that impair persuasion, leading to an inverted-U relationship. This research suggests that self-referencing can increase elaboration, initially enhancing persuasion based on strong arguments, but later reduces persuasion when elaboration is too high, either from too much self-referencing[187] or from self-referencing in addition to other elaboration enhancements.[188]

Different streams of research evoke self-referencing by eliciting autobiographical memories, defined as the recollection of earlier events in one's life.[189-191] In these studies, self-referencing does not enhance product elaboration, but rather distracts attention away from and eliminates the differential effects of strong versus weak arguments. Thinking about the self is shown to be an attention-consuming task. With an increase in self-focus, attention to the environment diminishes, reducing the interference of encoding new information.[192][193] More attention is directed towards the autobiographical episode, while thoughts about product features decline.

In the autobiographical memory studies, persuasion is still enhanced as a result of self-referencing, but the effect is due to the transfer of emotion or affect that occurs when the link between the brand and the autobiographical memory is made explicit in the ad message. When participants recall autobiographical memories, they generate positive affect, which is linked to the brand. From this research, it appears that an important aspect of self-referent processing is its affective power. Over time, the majority of autobiographical memories have strong affective associations built into them, which may help explain why highly affective incidents or autobiographical moments are remembered best.[194]

OPTIMAL DISTINCTIVENESS THEORY

The optimal distinctiveness model posits that human beings are characterized by two opposing needs that govern the relationship between the self-concept and membership in social groups.[195] The first is a need for assimilation and inclusion, a desire for belonging that motivates immersion in social groups. The second is a need for differentiation from others that operates in opposition to the need for immersion. As group membership becomes more and more inclusive, the need for inclusion is satisfied but the need for differentiation is activated; conversely, as inclusiveness decreases, the differentiation need is reduced but the need for inclusion is activated. These competing needs hold each other in check, assuring that interests at one level are not consistently sacrificed to interests at the other. According to the model, the two opposing motives produce an emergent characteristic – the capacity for social identification with distinctive groups that satisfies both needs simultaneously.

The basic premise of the optimal distinctiveness model is that the two identity needs (inclusion/assimilation and differentiation/distinctiveness) are independent of each other and work in opposition to form group identification. More specifically, this model proposes that social identities are selected and activated to the extent that they help achieve a balance between the needs for inclusion and for differentiation in any given social context. Optimal identities are those that satisfy the need for inclusion within the in-group and simultaneously serve the need for differentiation through distinctions between the in-group and out-group. In the original statement of the theory, leading researcher Marilynn Brewer tried to map the opposing drives and the point of equilibrium, as shown in Figure 4.[196]

Researchers widely consider the inclusion-need, the differentiation-need or both as fundamental to self and identity.[197-200] The idea that individuals prefer a balance between their needs for inclusion and differentiation is not novel. Rather, this notion is the basis for Uniqueness Theory[201] as well as for a number of theories of individuation[202-205] where the needs for inclusion and distinctiveness are seen as being met by comparisons with other individuals. Optimal Distinctiveness Theory differs from the other motivational theories in that the balance between inclusion and differentiation is achieved at the group level, through identification with groups that are both sufficiently inclusive and sufficiently distinct to meet both needs simultaneously.

In effect, optimal social identities involve shared distinctiveness.[206] [207] Individuals will resist being identified with social categorizations that are either too inclusive or too differentiating but will define themselves in terms of social identities that are optimally distinctive. Equilibrium is maintained by correcting for deviations from optimality. A situation in which a person is overly individuated will excite the need for inclusion, motivating the person to adopt a more inclusive social identity. Conversely, situations that create feelings of de-individuation tend to activate the need for differentiation, resulting in a search for more exclusive or distinct identities.

Although hypotheses derived from Optimal Distinctiveness Theory have been tested by different researchers in different contexts, some aspects of the theory are frequently misunderstood. The model does not suggest that optimal distinctiveness is a property of some groups rather than others and that individuals directly seek identification with these optimal groups. Rather, it sees optimality as a product of differential activation of the opposing motives for inclusion and differentiation and group properties that determine its level of inclusiveness and distinctiveness. This leads to three principles that are essential to understanding optimal distinctiveness.

First, optimal distinctiveness is context specific. Context affects both the activation of motives or needs and the relative distinctiveness of specific social categories. For example, in the context of a marketing conference, group identity as a marketer is inclusive but not optimally distinctive. In this context, shared identity as a market researcher is both sufficiently inclusive and differentiating. However, at a general business conference, group identity as a marketer is both inclusive and distinctive, and any sub-disciplinary group membership would be excessively differentiating.

Second, optimal distinctiveness is a dynamic equilibrium. Even within a given context, optimality is not necessarily fixed, because inclusion and differentiation motives are also subject to temporal influences and change over time. For example, when an individual first joins a new social group, inclusion and assimilation needs are likely to be particularly salient. At this stage, the new group member will be concerned that the in-group is sufficiently inclusive and broadly defined that they clearly fall within the group boundaries. Over time, however, when inclusion has been sufficiently established, differentiation motives are more likely to be activated and group members become more concerned that the in-group boundaries are defined so that the in-group can be clearly differentiated within its social context.

Third, identity motives vary across situation, culture and individuals. Asking "how strong an individual's inclusion motive is" is like asking how strong the individual's hunger motivation is. Like any need or drive, inclusion and differentiation motives vary as a function of current levels of satiation or deprivation. However, individuals may differ in how sensitive they are to changes in levels of inclusiveness.

The model as depicted in Figure 4 has four important parameters. These include the height (intercept) of the need for differentiation, the height (intercept) of the need for inclusion, the negative slope of the need for inclusion and the positive slope of the need for differentiation. Of these four, one is presumed to be fixed. The intercept (zero activation) of the need for differentiation is assumed to be at the point of complete individuation (the endpoint of the inclusiveness dimension). All of the other parameters vary; any changes in the intercept or slope of the inclusion drive or the slope of the differentiation drive will alter the point of equilibrium that represents an optimal identity. This model is just one representation that contains all possible variations in these parameters, and differences across situations, cultures and individuals can be represented in terms of variation in the slopes of the two drives (which can vary independently).[208] Again, the overall point is to emphasize that optimal distinctiveness is not a fixed property of groups or individuals, but a consequence of motivational dynamics at both levels.

Another important clarification is that although perceived intragroup inclusion and perceived intragroup differentiation are necessarily oppositional, the extent to which groups are able to meet group members' needs for inclusion and differentiation may actually be positively related. As noted previously, the need for inclusion is met through assimilation within the group (intragroup inclusion), whereas the need for differentiation is met through comparisons between groups (intergroup differentiation). Thus, it is possible for groups to be high on both dimensions, and indeed, to the extent that individuals pursue membership in optimally distinct groups in order to be both included and distinctive, evidence should indicate that greater perceived intergroup differentiation is positively associated with greater perceived intragroup inclusion.

In summary, Optimal Distinctiveness Theory stipulates that individuals are motivated by two fundamental and competing human needs and that individuals can simultaneously meet these needs by identifying with moderately inclusive group memberships. Such group memberships meet the need for inclusion within the group and the need for differentiation between groups. Furthermore, although the needs are necessarily oppositional, the extent to which groups are able to meet group members' needs for inclusion and differentiation may actually be positively related when inclusion is met within and differentiation is met between groups. Marketers can use Optimal Distinctiveness Theory to increase their understanding of Latinos and other multicultural consumers in the U.S.

ADVERTISING IN A MULTICULTURAL AMERICA

There is value in advertising to a segment of the Latino population in-culture (i.e., leveraging Spanish and consumer insights that are different from the mainstream). In fact, marketing to foreign-born Latinos in Spanish has been shown to increase media ROI based on a number of studies. As discussed in Chapter 3, our extensive research based on Nielsen C3 data confirms that Spanish-language advertising does not reach all Latinos in the United States, and Latinos are not linguistically homogeneous in their programming interests. Our Nativity-Based View research has shown that "where you are born" is a better predictor of media consumption than "language" across all U.S. Latinos. Marketers, as a result, are better off using Spanish-language advertising to engage a foreign-born Latino audience and considering media vehicles other than the traditional Spanish-language broadcast to reach a younger, more bicultural U.S.-born Latino demographic.

Although research on the multicultural population continues to lag compared to the non-Latino White mainstream, Nielsen has been exemplary over the years in measuring the viewership and engagement of Latinos and other multicultural consumers. Its landmark study conducted with Univision in 2017 and their follow up in 2020 found Spanish-language television ROI to have increased by 40 percent from 2017 to 2020.[209] A meta-analysis across a number of Nielsen marketing mix studies was used to investigate the drivers of higher ROI across Spanish Language advertising campaigns. The study included results across the marketing efforts of more than 50 projects over the past three years with clients in a wide variety of industries that assessed the performance of advertising in Spanish-language media. The assessment included brands in CPG (food, beverage, beauty, confection, household goods), financial services, insurance, telecom, cable and retail. The study attributed the following success factors to its findings: (1) investing in Latino advertising over time versus a short duration; (2) developing curated content; (3) having culturally relevant messaging that resonates with the Latino culture; and (4) executing campaigns with consistent frequency.[210] In addition, the study found that corporations that invested over $1 million in reaching U.S. Latinos saw the highest returns in their media investment.[211]

In a separate study conducted by Nielsen, Univision and Starcom's SMG Multicultural,[212] the impact of English- versus Spanish-language advertising was studied among 227 participants who self-identified as Latino, were between the ages of 21-34, spoke Spanish and English and were a mix of foreign- and U.S.-born. To determine the impact that language plays when advertising to bilingual consumers, the study measured consumer reactions to four ads (including Heineken Tiger), covering different categories that aired in both English and Spanish. Bilingual Latino Millennials' reactions to television ads were measured by Nielsen's proprietary consumer neuroscience technology. When comparing the neurological effectiveness of the identical or nearly identical advertisements in both languages, the Spanish version consistently performed the same or better than its English counterpart. Of the ads tested, no English ad performed significantly better than the same ad in Spanish.

Overall, the Spanish-language advertising did a better job of connecting with bicultural Latino Millennials across different scenarios, particularly when the ads' content was emotional in nature. Ads featuring social interaction were generally more emotionally engaging and memorable for bicultural Latino Millennials in Spanish than in English. Branding sequences were more effective in Spanish than in English. The study also found that Spanish-language advertising resonated better in the context of television programming. Spanish ads were more emotionally engaging when aired within a Spanish program than English ads within English programming. Similarly, emotional engagement for bicultural Latino Millennials decreased with English-language ads regardless of the programming language.

NBCU, Industry's parent company, is the other television network that has conducted a great deal of research on the viability of targeting Latinos in-language. There is a misconception in the marketplace that Spanish-language television is less effective for Latinos than English-language television. In 2018, NBCU and MAGNA conducted a joint study to better understand whether ads are more effective in Spanish than English. The study surveyed English- and Spanish-language respondents (with a booster sample for Latino respondents) who were asked to choose what content they wanted to watch and randomly inserted either "total market" ads or Spanish-language ads in the usual ad pods.[213]

As shown in Table 4.1, the study found that ads are more effective when the ad message leveraged culture. Compared to "total market" ads in English, "culture-first" ads were found to connect with the Latino culture and were perceived as more relevant, more informative, more entertaining and more easily understood.[214] The differences across three generational Latino segments were noticeable. The research found that when messaging Latinos, culture-first ads create stronger emotional responses and deeper cultural connections between the consumer and the brand.

The study is significant for number reasons. Over the last decade, many advertising agencies and clients have reduced their in-language marketing efforts or eliminated them, believing that they could reach Latinos in English-language media. The study shows that a "one and done" marketing strategy is an oversimplification, and that ethnic marketing is a viable opportunity. In fact, the study found that total market ads fell short among Latinos, and that ads that connected with Latinos on a cultural level elicited more emotion and drove key brand KPIs compared to non-culture-first messaging.[215]

THE FOUR-QUADRANT MODEL OF CULTURAL MARKETING

To help corporate America navigate a multicultural majority, in this section, I introduce the Four-Quadrant Model of Cultural Marketing (see Figure 4.1). This framework outlines the evolution of marketing communications in the United States since the mid 1960s. Although the business landscape is dynamic and complex, and a 2x2 matrix has its limitations, the proposed model is nevertheless quite robust in capturing the nuances of consumers and a number of marketing approaches.

Quadrant One reflects clients and agencies with the least amount of expertise in targeting multicultural consumers. This quadrant covers a period of time when many of the pioneers in Latino marketing came on the scene and the initial paradigmatic rules of cultural marketing were created. Corporations either ran their general market campaigns in English and believed they were reaching all consumers, or they translated their English-language ad campaigns into Spanish in an effort to reach key ethnic segments in select media verticals. The unforeseen problem was that some translations were ineffective or even offensive. Translations are the least strategic approach because they do not account for different consumer insights or communication strategies that are needed to maximize effectiveness when targeting different audiences. As such, these translation issues provided ethnic ad agencies the opportunity to develop "a better way" to market to all multicultural consumers, Latinos, African Americans and Asians.

Quadrant Two addresses the communication problems of Quadrant One by giving rise to a new marketing approach, the adaptation of general market advertising in which ethnic agencies communicated the general market strategy in a way that is culturally relevant. Popularized in the early 1990s, adaptations are one form of in-culture marketing. An example of an adaptation is Allstate's Mayhem campaign, which has been running for more than a decade. Stemming from the success of its national ad campaign, Allstate introduced its Mala Suerte character to Latino audiences to highlight the protection, value and peace of mind that Allstate provides when bad things happen. The word "mayhem" has no literal translation in Spanish, which led Allstate to create Mala Suerte to resonate more directly with Latino consumers. ("Mala suerte" translates to bad luck.) According to Allstate, consumer research showed that many Latinos blame accidents on fate or bad luck and are more likely to find fault with circumstances rather than a person who may have done something wrong.

No matter the popularity or awards, the adaptation approach has significant limitations. The biggest downside to creative adaptations is that the output, no matter how creative, is driven by general market insights. Oftentimes, ethnic agencies are asked by the mainstream agency and/or clients whether the general market campaign works for a given multicultural segment. With fear of losing a business opportunity, ethnic agencies have done their best to accommodate these restrictions and develop a synergistic campaign to the general market. But adaptations are also tactical and designed to support the general market advertising efforts. They are not built around unique consumer insights that meet lower-funnel objectives. I would discourage general market agencies from asking whether their campaign can be adapted into Spanish. This typically leads to a self-fulfilling prophecy and to sub-optimal strategic work.

Quadrant Three has defined Latino marketing for more than three decades. It is the closest to executing a pure segmentation strategy, which is based on developing an original strategy and executions with different multicultural consumers. This is the other form of in-culture marketing. Brands in this Quadrant believe in the power of in-culture marketing. The large corporations that spend with in-language publishers can be found in this quadrant.

Companies in Quadrant Four have a contemporary view of the demography and have aligned their marketing capabilities to it. Marketing in Quadrant Four is based on multicultural insights that drive business performance. Corporations in this quadrant do not view multicultural marketing in a silo. They see the multicultural consumer as their core customer, front and center of the New Mainstream. This perceptual change is not small. In fact, I have likened this mindset shift as comparable to a paradigm shift. It is that significant and fundamental. In Quadrant Four, consumer insights reflect the multicultural population, and marketing efforts are communicated in English.

Quadrant Four speaks to a new model that few corporations have adopted at this point in time. Category leaders base their brand strategy on the multicultural population and develop marketing communication plans in English. I use Procter & Gamble as an example because I believe Mr. Prichard's quote at the beginning of this chapter speaks to the heart of the changes that more companies need to make: Companies are not doing marketing unless they are doing multicultural marketing in the 21st century. This is another way of saying that mainstream marketing needs to change due to the increasingly diverse demographic landscape. Today and in the future, optimal marketing will exist in Quadrants Three and Four. They live side-by-side and for good reason. This chapter proposes that understanding your consumer through science is at the heart of marketing excellence. No single approach can address the complexities and consumer nuances, which is why Quadrants Three and Four are the best combination in driving marketing effectiveness in a multicultural America. Any company that promotes one Quadrant over another is promoting its business model. Corporations should take a consumer-centric approach and invest in both.

CONCLUSIONS AND IMPLICATIONS

Big Data allows marketers to be agnostic. Moving forward, marketers must abandon the conceptual models of the 20th century for models built with data science. By the same token, marketers must challenge the heuristics that once helped kick-start Latino marketing more than three decades ago with new mental models that align with a multicultural America. All of this is possible when there is a willingness to follow the data.

Quadrant Three is the silo for in-language marketing. It is where in-language publishers and ethnic ad agencies partner to meet the needs of specific ethnic segments. Quadrant Four, on the other hand, redefines marketing in a multicultural America. It is based on the notion that America is a multicultural majority, and marketers must view the multicultural population as the New Mainstream. This book proposes that optimal growth will occur when corporations adopt approaches in Quadrants Three and Four simultaneously.

The proposed shifts challenge the popular "total market"

advertising approach. Although this methodology initially provided brands with a centralized process that drove marketing efficiencies, total market is ineffectual. Marketing without multicultural consumers front and center in today's mainstream is off-strategy. The opportunity, therefore, lies in embracing a total market strategy with multicultural consumers at its core, which this book proposes will become the de facto marketing standard in the 21st century. This chapter also proposes that Self-Referencing and Optimal Distinctiveness Theory can be used to help understand multicultural consumers. Corporate America must develop new marketing strategies (like they did with the rise of Millennials) to grow their business with a multicultural mainstream. Corporations will need to undergo The Big Shift, not only in how they view the landscape, but in how they manage their business, organizations and key stakeholders.

Figure 4
Optimal Distinctiveness Theory

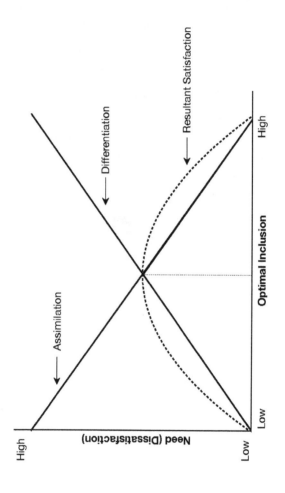

Source: Brewer, M. and Roccas, S. (2001). Individual Values, Social Identity, and Optimal Distinctiveness. in C. Sedikides & M. B. Brewer (Eds.), Individual Self, Relational Self, Collective Self: 219-237. Philadelphia: Psychology Press/Taylor & Francis.

Figure 4.1
The Four-Quadrant Model of Cultural Marketing

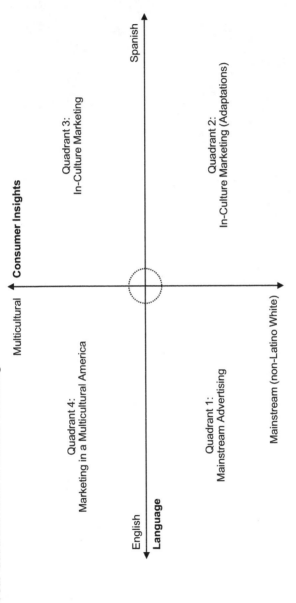

Consumer Insights

Spanish

Multicultural

Quadrant 3:
In-Culture Marketing

Quadrant 2:
In-Culture Marketing (Adaptations)

Quadrant 4:
Marketing in a Multicultural America

Quadrant 1:
Mainstream Advertising

Mainstream (non-Latino White)

English

Language

Source: The Center for Multicultural Science.

Table 4
Spanish-Language TV and English-Language TV Content Effectiveness for U.S. Latinos by Generational Level

	First Generation		Second Generation		Third+ Generation	
	SLTV	ELTV	SLTV	ELTV	SLTV	ELTV
Connects to My Culture	62%	47%	63%	51%	61%	50%
Relevant	69%	58%	73%	54%	72%	59%
Informative	78%	77%	78%	63%	66%	55%
Entertaining	76%	74%	73%	57%	75%	57%
Clear Communication	91%	89%	87%	80%	88%	77%

Source: NBCU and MAGNA (2018). Accessed on July 2, 2020: https://together.nbcuni.com/article/total-market-fallacy/. English-Language Television (ELTV): First Generation: N=71. Second Generation: N=163. Third Generation: N=175. Spanish-Language Television (SLTV): First Generation: N=105. Second Generation: N=155. Third Generation: N=60.

CHAPTER FOUR ENDNOTES

[166] Vizard, S. (2018). P&G: If You Aren't Doing Multicultural Marketing, You Aren't Doing Marketing. *MarketingWeek*. Accessed June 25, 2020: https://www.marketingweek.com/pg-multicultural-marketing/

[167] Vespa, J., Medina, L., and Armstrong, D. (2020). Demographic Turning Points for the United States: Population Projections for 2020 to 2060. Current Population Reports. P25-1144. Accessed on March 3, 2020: https://www.census.gov/content/dam/Census/library/publications/2020/demo/p25-1144.pdf

[168] Rogers, T., Kuiper, N., and Kirker, W. (1977). Self-Reference and the Encoding of Personal Information. *Journal of Personality and Social Psychology*. 35(1): 677-688.

[169] Burnkrant, R. and Unnava, H. (1995). Effects of Self-Referencing on Persuasion. *Journal of Consumer Research*. 22(1): 17-26.

[170] Mehler, M. (2011). The Effects of Self-Referencing and Mood on Information Processing. Unpublished Thesis. San Jose, CA. Accessed July 1, 2020: https://scholarworks.sjsu.edu/cgi/viewcontent.cgi?article=5101&context=etd_theses

[171] Brewer, M. (1991). The Social Self: On Being the Same and Different at the Same Time. *The Society for Personality and Social Psychology*. 17(5): 475-482.

[172] Leonardelli, G., Pickett, C., and Brewer, M. (2010). Optimal Distinctiveness Theory: A Framework for Social Identity, Social Cognition, and Intergroup Relations. In M. P. Zanna & J. M. Olson (Eds.), Advances in Experimental Social Psychology. *Advances in Experimental Social Psychology*. 43(1): 63-113.

[173] Beniflah, J. and Hughes, B. (2016). An Industry Response: There *is* a Better Way to Target the U.S. Hispanic Television Audience. *Journal of Cultural Marketing Strategy*. 1(2): 170-179.

[174] Kotler, P. (2000). Marketing Management. Upper Saddle River: Prentice Hall.

[175] Debevec, K. and Romeo, J. (1992). Self-Referent Processing in Perceptions of Verbal and Visual Commercial Information. *Journal of Consumer Psychology*. 1(1): 83-102.

[176] Klein, S. and Loftus, J. (1988). The Nature of Self-Referent Encoding: The Contributions of Elaborative and Organizational Processes. *Journal of Personality and Social Psychology*. 55(July): 5-11.

[177] Rogers, T., Kuiper, N., and Kirker, W. (1977). Self-Reference and the Encoding of Personal Information. *Journal of Personality and Social Psychology.* 35(September): 677-688.

[178] Greenwald, A. and Banjai, M. (1989). The Self as Memory System: Powerful but Ordinary. *Journal of Personality and Social Psychology.* 57(July): 41-54.

[179] Klein, S., Loftus, J., and Schell, T. (1994). Repeated Testing: A Technique for Assessing the Roles of Elaborative and Organizational Processing in the Representation of Social Knowledge. *Journal of Personality and Social Psychology.* 66(5): 830-839.

[180] Burnkrant, R. and Unnava, R. (1995). Effects of Self-Referencing on Persuasion. *Journal of Consumer Research.* 22(June): 17-26.

[181] Debevec, K. and Romeo, J. (1992). Self-Referent Processing in Perceptions of Verbal and Visual Commercial Information. *Journal of Consumer Psychology.* 1(1): 83-102.

[182] Sujan, M., Bettman, J. and Baumgartner, H. (1993). Influencing Consumer Judgments Using Autobiographical Memories: A Self-Referencing Perspective. *Journal of Marketing Research.* 30(4): 422-436.

[183] Burnkrant, R. and Unnava, R. (1989). Self-Referencing: A Strategy for Increasing Processing of Message Content. *Personality and Social Psychology Bulletin.* 15(December): 628-638.

[184] Meyers-Levy, J. and Peracchio, L. (1996). Moderators of the Impact of Self-Reference on Persuasion. *Journal of Consumer Research.* 22(March): 408-423.

[185] Burnkrant, R. and Unnava, R. (1995). Effects of Self-Referencing on Persuasion. *Journal of Consumer Research.* 22(June): 17-26.

[186] Anand, P. and Sternthal, B. (1989). Strategies for Designing Persuasive Messages: Deductions from the Resource Matching Hypothesis in *Cognitive and Affective Responses to Advertising*, eds. Patricia Cafferata and Alice M. Tybout, 135-159.

[187] Meyers-Levy, J. and Peracchio, L. (1996). Moderators of the Impact of Self-Reference on Persuasion. *Journal of Consumer Research.* 22(March): 408-423.

[188] Burnkrant, R. and Unnava, R. (1995). Effects of Self-Referencing on Persuasion. *Journal of Consumer Research.* 22(June): 17-26.

[189] Sujan, M., Bettman, J., and Baumgartner, H. (1993). Influencing Consumer Judgments Using Autobiographical Memories: A Self-Referencing Perspective. *Journal of Marketing Research.* 30(4): 422-436.

[190] Baumgartner, H., Sujan, M. and Bettman, J. (1992). Autobiographical Memories, Affect, and Consumer Information Processing. *Journal of Consumer Psychology.* 1: 53-82.

[191] Baddeley, A. (1990). Recollection and Autobiographical Memory. Chapter 12 in Human Memory, Needham Heights: Allyn and Bacon.

[192] Mick, D. (1992). Levels of Subjective Comprehension in Advertising Processing and Their Relations to Ad Perceptions, Attitudes, and Memory. *Journal of Consumer Research.* 18(4): 411-424.

[193] Sujan, M., Bettman, J. and Baumgartner, H. (1993). Influencing Consumer Judgments Using Autobiographical Memories: A Self-Referencing Perspective. *Journal of Marketing Research.* 30(4): 422-436.

[194] Brewer, W. (1986). What is Autobiographical Memory? in Autobiographical Memory, David C. Rubin, ed., New York: Cambridge University Press, 25-49.

[195] Brewer, M. (1991). The Social Self: On Being The Same and Different at The Same Time. *Personality & Social Psychology Bulletin.* 17(5): 475-482.

[196] Ibid.

[197] Baumeister, R. and Leary, M. (1995). The Need to belong: Desire for Interpersonal Attachments as a Fundamental Human Motivation. *Psychological Bulletin.* 117(3): 497-529.

[198] Fiske, S. (2004). Social Beings: A Core Motives Approach to Social Psychology. New York: Wiley.

[199] Maslow, A. (1943). A Theory of Human Motivation. *Psychological Review.* 50: 370-396.

[200] Vignoles, V., Regalia, C., Manzi, C., Golledge, J., and Scabini, E. (2006). Beyond Self- Esteem: Influence of Multiple Motives on Identity Construction. *Journal of Personality and Social Psychology.* 90(2): 308-333.

[201] Snyder, C. and Fromkin, H. (1980). *Uniqueness: The Human Pursuit of Difference.* New York: Plenum Press.

[202] Codol, J.-P. (1975). On the So-Called "Superior Conformity of the Self" Behavior: Twenty Experimental Investigations. *European Journal of Social Psychology.* 5(4): 457-501.

[203] Lemaine, G. (1974). Social Differentiation and Social Originality. *European Journal of Social Psychology.* 4: 17-52.

[204] Maslach, C. (1974). Social and Personal Bases of Individuation. *Journal of Personality and Social Psychology.* 29: 411-425.

[205] Ziller, R. (1964). Individuation and Socialization. *Human Relations.* 17: 341-360.

[206] Brewer, M. and Silver, M. (2000). Group Distinctiveness, Social Identification, and Collective Mobilization. In S. Stryker, T. J. Owens, & R. W. White (Eds.), Self, Identity, and Social Movements: 153-171. Minneapolis: University of Minnesota Press.

[207] Stapel, D. and Marx, D. (2007). Distinctiveness is Key: How Different Types of Self-Other Similarity Moderate Social Comparison Effects. *Personality and Social Psychology Bulletin.* 33: 439-448.

[208] Brewer, M. and Roccas, S. (2001). Individual Values, Social Identity, and Optimal Distinctiveness. in C. Sedikides & M. B. Brewer (Eds.), Individual Self, Relational Self, Collective Self: 219-237. Philadelphia: Psychology Press/Taylor & Francis.

[209] Ruiz, R., (2020). The Secrets to Higher ROI in Spanish-Language TV. MediaVillage. Accessed: July 12, 2020. https://www.mediavillage.com/article/secrets-of-spanish-language-advertising-20-an-opportunity-for-todays-marketers/

[210] Nielsen, (2017). The Secrets to Spanish-language TV ROI. Accessed: July 12, 2020. https://www.nielsen.com/us/en/insights/report/2017/the-secrets-to-spanish-language-tv-roi/

[211] Ibid.

[212] Nielsen, (2014). The Bilingual Brain: Maximizing Impact with English- and Spanish-Speaking Millennials. Accessed: July 12, 2020. https://www.nielsen.com/wp-content/uploads/sites/3/2019/04/bilingual-brain-report.pdf

[213] NBCU and MAGNA (2018). Total Market Fallacy: Using In-Culture Marketing to Drive Your Growth with Hispanics. Accessed on July 2, 2020: https://together.nbcuni.com/article/total-market-fallacy/

[214] Ibid.

[215] Ibid.

CHAPTER
FIVE

You've heard the popular expression: "If you can't measure it, you can't manage it." This famous quote, attributed to management guru Peter Drucker 40 years ago, is more relevant than ever. In this chapter, I propose that aligning new measures to a changing demographic landscape is key to a firm's sustainable competitive advantage. Over the last two decades, the demographic shifts of our country have posed significant challenges to marketers in virtually every business category. The U.S. Census estimates that Latinos, African Americans, Asians and other ethnic and racial groups will outnumber non-Latino Whites by 2043.[216] So the next 20 years look just as uncertain and disruptive as the last two decades. The so-called demographic tipping point is really more symbolic given that nearly 70 percent of the country's largest cities today are more racially and ethnically diverse than they were a decade ago.[217] The fear that non-Latino Whites will be replaced or left behind in a country where they are slowly becoming the minority has helped flame the recent wave of White nationalism.[218] Leading marketers, nevertheless, understand that without measuring a multicultural America, their businesses will suffer. Latinos, African Americans and Asians are the New Mainstream. They know the importance of staying ahead of key demographic trends and advancing new marketing and measurement strategies to address an ever-evolving business landscape.

This chapter lays out a simple tenet: if we truly believe that the mainstream is multicultural, we must measure the New Mainstream not in aggregate, but by ethnicity and race. In this chapter, I present a metric called the Ethnicity-Race View (ERV), which measures everything that matters to marketers by ethnicity and race. Partnering with MAGNA, we publish 2018 and 2019 media spend by ethnicity and race, challenging prior studies that report media spend in aggregate and by language. Second, I discuss the applications of this metric and suggest how corporations can improve measurement, and ultimately their performance in the New Mainstream. We are all chartering new waters so things may be a bit choppy at first. Mental models, which I discuss in the following chapter, are difficult to change. When we challenge our deeply engrained worldviews, only then can we begin to broaden our perspective, which allows us to think and act differently.

THE ETHNICITY-RACE VIEW

Measuring the world by ethnicity and race is not a novel concept. The U.S. Census enumerates our country's population across Latinos, African Americans, Asians and other ethnic and racial groups. The U.S. Bureau of Labor Statistics measures and reports key economic variables (consumer expenditures, unemployment rate, educational attainment and many others) by ethnicity and race. Virtually all corporations, today, recognize the changing demographic landscape, and market their products and services across different customer segments. So why introduce a metric like the Ethnicity-Race View (ERV) when companies have already been using this measure for some time?

We are not introducing a new metric, per se. We are advocating that companies permanently adopt this methodology moving forward.[219] The U.S. Census and the Bureau of Labor Statistics provide data across a number of variables, which, today, include ethnicity and race. But it wasn't always the case. The U.S. Census was established in 1790 to provide Congress with an enumeration of the country's population whose methodology and classifications have evolved over time.[220] Interestingly, it was until 1970 when the White House instructed the Secretary of Commerce to add a Hispanic self-identification question into the U.S. Census. Before then, "Mexicans" were enumerated in 1930 for the first time but were subsequently dropped for three decades until new measures were introduced in the 1970 Census.[221]

Blacks or African Americans have been a part of the U.S. Census, but their classification has changed nine times since 1790, the most of any racial group.[222] The Census expanded the classification of Asians eight times since 1860,[223] modified the taxonomy for Hawaiians seven times,[224] and Indians six times.[225] Race and ethnicity are social constructs and are susceptible to political, economic and social forces in our country.[226] [227]

Interestingly, the Bureau of Labor Statistics began measuring the unemployment rate for Whites in 1954,[228] African Americans in 1972,[229] Latinos in 1973,[230] and Asians in 2003.[231] It began measuring U.S. unemployment rate in aggregate in 1947.[232] The U.S. Census began measuring educational attainment for Whites and African Americans in 1940,[233] Latinos in 1974,[234] and Asians in 2003.[235] It began measuring educational attainment in aggregate in 1940.[236] The United States has always been a multicultural nation, but it hasn't always been measured as such. So, what can corporate America learn from all of this?

It is important that all corporations adopt an Ethnicity-Race View given that non-Latino Whites are slowly becoming the minority in our country. The dramatic changes in our country's demography warrants that companies understand how they are doing with all consumers, not just with Whites. The top five cities today are driven by multicultural consumers.[237] If companies are measuring their market performance against the total population in aggregate, they fail to understand who's driving their business. But don't companies today measure what matters by ethnicity and race?

In many cases, the answer is yes, but not all measurement companies do. The largest digital measurement companies in the United States currently do not provide granular measures on Latinos and Asians. Sales measurement companies which report shopper marketing (scanner) data, provide sales estimates by ethnicity and race, which do not reflect actual sales data. They are sales estimates which end up being used by America's top companies to calculate advertising and marketing ROI. These estimates can produce unreliable calculations, negatively impacting revenue and sales projections. As such, the field of marketing and sales measurement in the United States is ripe for disruptive innovation.

These types of measurement problems are not new, have been well-documented and tend to reflect legacy issues that continue to impact sales measurement of multicultural shoppers.[238] This is why adopting an Ethnicity-Race View is so important. It is more than just a construct that measures the world by ethnicity and race. It is a methodology that requires a certain mental model that aligns with a country that is inching towards a multicultural majority.

There are a number of reasons why our country's marketing measurement system needs a reboot. Measurement tends to lag marketplace changes,[239] and measurement companies tend to retrofit new measures that respond to new market opportunities, business priorities and changing demographics. In other words, they tend to be market-driven instead of driving-the-market.[240] Second, some argue that ethnocentrism plays a role in how companies see the world which impacts their measurement priorities. Third, some companies know they have blind spots in their datasets, and they chose to do nothing about them in the short-term. Fourth, core competencies can lead to core rigidities, which speaks to the difficulty in adapting to a changing environment.[241]

Although virtually all marketers today understand that the business landscape is constantly in flux, there is no consensus on what marketing looks like in multicultural America. Marketplace success is inherently a function of many factors, including organizational capabilities,[242] strategic execution,[243] a company's human resources,[244] and a multitude of strategic factors[245] which vary across companies. Corporations differ not only in what they see, but in how they chose to respond to environmental threats and opportunities. Corporations, as a result, tend fall into three categories: leaders, followers or laggards.[246] As such, corporate America is not homogeneous in its market orientation and marketing capabilities, and is not ready for a multicultural America.[247]

So, what creates these blind spots and how can companies avoid them? Companies should begin by being open to different worldviews and perspectives. As discussed in Chapter 1, marketers have operationalized Latinos as a culturally homogeneous group, bound by within-group similarities. Moving forward, marketers have the opportunity to simultaneously adopt a research design based on similarities *and* differences between-groups.[248] This is an area which has the most potential to fuel growth for companies in the 21st century.

As the demographic landscape continues to evolve, the world of measurement will need to change with it. The next section of this chapter outlines advertising media spend in 2018 and 2019 using the Ethnicity-Race View. For the last two years, this methodology has helped brands measure how much of their advertising reaches ethnic and racial segments in the United States across different media.

ADVERTISING MEDIA SPEND

If the New Mainstream is multicultural, measurement must evolve accordingly. In 2018, the Center for Multicultural Science and MAGNA teamed up to publish advertising media spend by ethnicity and race for the first time in the history of the advertising industry. Advertising spend has traditionally been aggregated across all ethnic and racial groups, making it difficult to understand the contribution that each multicultural population group has on advertising spend.

In 2018, corporations in the United States spent a little more than $100 billion targeting consumers with digital media.[249] By 2019, digital media spend had grown almost by 20 percent, to $119.2 billion.[250] Table 5 outlines digital media spend for 2018 and 2019 as a digital discipline.[251] Search continues to make up 45 percent of all digital media spend in the United States.[252] Social media makes up about 28 percent of all digital media spend in this country.[253] And not surprisingly, video is the third largest category in digital media, at 12 percent of total digital media spend.[254]

Table 5.1 shows the percentage of digital media spend in

2018 for all ethnic in racial groups in the United States and compares it to the population percentage for these consumers.[255] Although non-Latino Whites make up about 60 percent of the U.S. population, they contribute 66 percent of all digital spend in this country. Latinos, who make up 18 percent of the population, represent 14 percent of all digital spend in the United States. And for African American and Asian consumers, the percentage of media spend for each segment closely aligns to their population percentage. Table 5.2 breaks down digital media spend by ethnicity and race across six different types of digital media.[256] Comparing media spend percentages to population percentages is just one way of looking at media spend. It should not be used as a sole metric to determine how much corporations should invest with specific consumers. Corporations need to determine the right spend for their business. There is no evidence that a one-size-fits-all media allocation formula drives business growth or ROI for any particular brand or industry.

Linear television is another billion-dollar category but declining slowly each year. In 2018, companies spent an estimated $42.1 billion in linear television and an estimated $41.5 billion in 2019.[257] As shown in Table 5.3, cable television makes up approximately 60 percent of linear television spend in the United States.[258] English-broadcast television is roughly a $13 billion business, declining slightly year-to-year.[259] Syndication ranks third of all linear television, estimated at $1.8 billion in 2019. Spanish-language broadcast television is an estimated $1.2 billion category, last year.[260] This figure is starkly different from what is reported annually in the *AdAge Hispanic Fact Pack*, which only accounts for Spanish-language media spend.[261] As outlined in Table 5.4, approximately 65 percent of linear television was spent reaching non-Latino Whites, almost 18 percent to African Americans, 13 percent to Latinos, 3 percent to Asians, and 2 percent to All Other viewers.[262] There is always an opportunity for brands to allocate their budgets more effectively and efficiently.

CONCLUSION

This chapter proposes that more granular measures are required as a result of a changing demography. New metrics will need to quantify the marketing world by ethnicity and race. I have called this approach the Ethnicity-Race View. The argument is straightforward. Corporations across all industries need to attribute their business outcomes to a multicultural America. Today, across the country's top cities, the majority of the population is multicultural.[263] Cities, like New York, are projecting a negative population growth rate of 1.5 percent over the next five years among non-Latino Whites; meaning that more non-Latino Whites deaths are expected to outnumber live births.[264] Other cities such as Los Angeles are seeing a marginal population growth rate (less than 1 percent) compared to the Latino, African American and Asian population segments. Companies interested to win now should be looking at their business through a multicultural marketing lens.[265] In roughly 25 years, the United States, as a nation, is projected to become a multicultural majority and all companies will have to effectively measure a multicultural marketplace.[266]

The argument to align measures to the changing demography is intuitive. Few will argue with this posit. The part of marketing where consensus is lacking is in strategy. The question of how to grow sales in a multicultural marketplace plagues most companies today. There is an additional reason for disaggregating aggregated data in measuring the New Mainstream. It has to do with a little-known phenomenon in the field of probability and statistics. The Simpson's Paradox is a phenomenon in which a trend appears in several different groups of data but disappears or reverses when these groups are combined.[267-269] This phenomenon appears every single day in business. For instance, the U.S. unemployment rate in 2019 was at a historically all-time low. When looking at the impact of unemployment on African Americans and Latinos, the unemployment rate for these two groups (6.1 percent and 4.3 percent, respectively)[270] was higher than the national average of 3.7 percent.[271] As shown in Figure 5, the unemployment rate for U.S. Latinos and African Americans has always been higher than non-Latino Whites in this country.[272] The unemployment rate for Asians, on the other hand, has almost always been lower than any other ethnic and racial group in the United States.[273] This example shows how aggregated data produces opposite findings that have significant economic implications – not just on the different population segments, but the country as a whole. Disaggregating the data by ethnicity and race allows economists and business executives to develop policies to address the specific issues impacting the various population segments. Furthermore, because economic growth is closely tied to population growth which is driven by the U.S. multicultural population, disaggregating CRM and other forms of data by ethnicity and race will help corporations develop more effective strategies in an increasingly diverse marketplace.

Table 5
Percentage of Digital Media Spend by Type and Year

	2018	2019
Search	45%	45%
Social	28%	31%
Video	12%	13%
Display	8%	6%
Other	4%	3%
Audio	3%	2%

Source: MAGNA estimates.

Table 5.1
Percentage of Digital Media Spend in 2018 and Population Percentage by Ethnicity and Race

	Spend %	Population %
Non-Latino White	65.9%	60.7%
Latino	14.3%	18.1%
African American	12.1%	13.4%
Asian	6.6%	5.8%
Other	1.1%	-

Source: MAGNA estimates. U.S. Census Bureau.

Table 5.2
Digital Media 2018 Spend by Type, Ethnicity and Race and Total

	Non-Latino White	Latino	African American	Asian
Search	66.9%	14.0%	11.5%	6.4%
Video	63.4%	14.1%	14.1%	7.0%
Display	65.8%	14.2%	12.0%	6.6%
Social	66.0%	14.2%	11.9%	6.7%
Other	62.3%	17.6%	12.1%	6.6%
Audio	62.4%	15.3%	14.3%	6.8%
Total	65.9%	14.3%	12.1%	6.6%

Source: MAGNA estimates.

Table 5.3
Linear Television Spend by Type, Year and Total

	2018	2019
National Cable	$25,408	$25,309
English Broadcast	$13,500	$13,182
Syndication	$1,911	$1,852
Spanish Broadcast	$1,284	$1,235
Total	$42,103	$41,478

Source: MAGNA estimates, (000).

Table 5.4
Percentage of Linear Television 2018 Percentage Spend by Type, Ethnicity, Race and Total

	Non-Latino White	Latino	African American	Asian	Other
National Cable	66.9%	8.5%	19.9%	2.1%	2.5%
English Broadcast	72.5%	6.4%	16.2%	2.9%	2.1%
Syndication	63.9%	7.1%	24.5%	2.3%	2.2%
Spanish Broadcast	1.8%	97.3%	0.06%	0.3%	-
Total	64.8%	12.5%	17.8%	2.9%	2.0%

Source: MAGNA estimates.

Figure 5
U.S. Unemployment Rate by Ethnicity and Race (1973-2020)

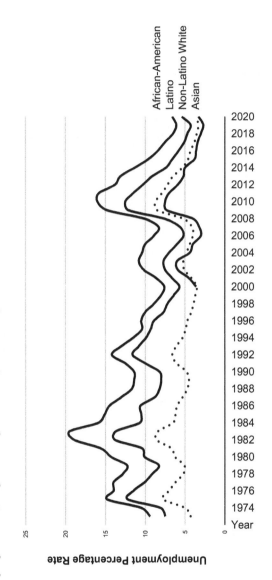

Source: Bureau of Labor Statistics; https://www.bls.gov/opub/reports/race-and-ethnicity/2018/home.htm (Chart 5), https://www.bls.gov/web/empsit/cpsee_e16.htm, https://www.bls.gov/cps/cpsaat06.pdf, https://www.bls.gov/cps/cps/cpsaat05.pdf

CHAPTER FIVE ENDNOTES

[216] U.S. Census Bureau, 2020.

[217] McPhillips, D. (2020). A New Analysis Finds Growing Diversity in U.S. Cities. U.S. News. Accessed on February 2, 2020: https://www.usnews.com/news/cities/articles/2020-01-22/americas-cities-are-becoming-more-diverse-new-analysis-shows

[218] Anti-Defamation League. (2019). Two Years Ago, They Marched in Charlottesville. Where Are They Now? Accessed on March 1, 2020: https://www.adl.org/blog/two-years-ago-they-marched-in-charlottesville-where-are-they-now

[219] Pratt, B., Hixson, L., and Jones, N. (Unknown). U.S. Census Population Updates. Measuring Race and Ethnicity Across the Decades: 1790-2010 Mapped to 1997 U.S. Office of Management and Budget Classification Standards. Accessed March 2, 2020: https://www.census.gov/data-tools/demo/race/MREAD_1790_2010.html

[220] Ibid.

[221] Ibid.

[222] Ibid. (Slaves in 1790; Slaves; Free Colored Persons in 1830; Black, Mulatto in 1870; Black, Mulatto, Quadroon, Octoroon in 1890; Black (Negro or of Negro Descent) in 1900; Black (Negro), Mulatto in 1910; Negro in 1930; Negro or Black in 1970; Black, African American or Negro in 2000.

[223] Ibid. (Chinese in 1860; Japanese in 1890; Filipino, Hindi and Korean in 1920; Vietnamese and Asian Indian in 1980, and Other Asian in 2000).

[224] Ibid. (Hawaiian and Part Hawaiian in 1960; Hawaiian in 1970; Hawaiian, Samoan, and Guamanian in 1980; Hawaiian, Samoan, Guamanian and Other Asian Pacific Islander in 1990; Native Hawaiian, Samoan, Guamanian or Chamorro, and Other Pacific Islander in 2000).

[225] Ibid. (Indian in 1870; Aleut, American Indian, Eskimo in 1960; American Indian and Alaska Native in 2000).

[226] Mallon, R. (2004). Passing, Traveling and Reality: Social Constructionism and the Metaphysics of Race. *Noûs*. 38(4): 644-673.

[227] Pierce, J. (2014). Review: Why Teaching About Race as a Social Construct Still Matters. *Sociological Forum*. 29(1): 259-264.

[228] Bureau of Labor Statistics, Series ID: LNS14000003.

[229] Bureau of Labor Statistics, Series ID: LNS14000006.

[230] Bureau of Labor Statistics, Series ID: LNS14000009.

[231] Bureau of Labor Statistics: Series ID: LNS14032183.

[232] Bureau of Labor Statistics, Series ID: LNU04000000.

[233] Bureau of Labor Statistics. CPS Historical Time Series Tables. Table A-2. Percent of People 25 Years and Over Who Have Completed High School or College, by Race, Hispanic Origin and Sex: Selected Years 1940 to 2019.

[234] Ibid.

[235] Ibid.

[236] Ibid.

[237] U.S. Census Bureau, 2020.

[238] Valdés, I. and Beniflah, J. (2014). Why Can't the Hispanic Market Get Its Fair Share of Investment? *AdAge*. Accessed on January 24, 2020: https://adage.com/article/the-big-tent/hispanic-market-fair-share-investment/238807

[239] Kantu, D. and Durbach, I. (2013). Unknown. Accessed on February 3, 2020: http://www.samra.co.za/wp-content/uploads/2013/05/Kantu-Durbach_Early-warning-systems-Research-Paper.pdf

[240] Hills, S. and Sarin, S. (2003). From Market Driven to Market Driving: An Alternate Paradigm for Marketing in High Technology Industries. *The Journal of Marketing Theory and Practice*. 11(3): 13-24.

[241] Leonard-Barton, D. (1992). Core capabilities and Core Rigidities: A Paradox in Managing New Product Development. *Strategic Management Journal*. 13(1) Special Issue Summer: 111-125.

[242] Celuch, K., Kasouf, C., and Peruvemba, V. (2002). The Effects of Perceived Market and Learning Orientation on Assessed Organizational Capabilities. *Industrial Marketing Management*. 31(6): 545-554.

[243] Hrebiniak, L. (2013). Making Strategy Work: Leading Effective Execution and Change. Upper Saddle River: Pearson Education, Inc.

[244] Kaplan, R. and Norton, D. (2008). The Execution Premium: Linking Strategy to Operations for Competitive Advantage. Boston: Harvard Business School Publishing Company.

[245] Porter, M. (2008). The Five Competitive Forces That Shape Strategy. *Harvard Business Review*. January 2008: 24-41.

[246] Coad, A. (2011). Appropriate Business Strategy for Leaders and Laggards. Industrial and Corporate Change. 20(4): 1049–1079.

[247] Beniflah, J. (2020). A Marketing Capabilities Assessment of U.S. Companies. Unpublished Pilot Study.

[248] Villarreal, R. and Blozis, S. (2015). The Importance of the Analytic Approach to the Multigroup Ethnic Identity Measure in the Study of Hispanic Media Behaviour. *The Journal of Cultural Marketing Strategy*. 1(1): 32-44.

[249] MAGNA estimates, 2018 and 2019.

[250] Ibid.

[251] Ibid.

[252] Ibid.

[253] Ibid.

[254] Ibid.

[255] MAGNA estimates, 2018.

[256] Ibid.

[257] MAGNA estimates, 2018 and 2019.

[258] Ibid.

[259] Ibid.

[260] Ibid.

[261] Hispanic Fact Pack. (2019). *AdAge*. New York: Crain Communications, Inc.

[262] MAGNA estimates, 2018.

[263] Easydemographics, Inc. Data is based on U.S. Census Bureau.

[264] Ibid.

[265] Ibid.

[266] Ibid.

[267] Simpson, E. (1951). The Interpretation of Interaction in Contingency Tables. *Journal of the Royal Statistical Society*. Series B. 13: 238-241.

[268] Yule, G. (1903). Notes on the Theory of Association of Attributes in Statistics. *Biometrika*. 2 (2): 121-134.

[269] Blyth, C. (1972). On Simpson's Paradox and the Sure-Thing Principle. *Journal of the American Statistical Association*. 67(338): 364-366.

[270] Bureau of Labor Statistics. (Unknown). Labor Force Statistics from the Current Population Survey. E-16 Unemployment Rates by Age, Sex, Race, and Hispanic or Latino Ethnicity. Accessed on March 2, 2020: https://www.bls.gov/web/empsit/cpsee_e16.htm

[271] Bureau of Labor Statistics. (Unknown). Labor Force Statistics from the Current Population Survey. Household Annual Data Averages. Employment Status of the Civilian Noninstitutional Population by Sex, Age, and Race. Accessed on Match 5, 2020: https://www.bls.gov/cps/cpsaat05.pdf

[272] Bureau of Labor Statistics Reports. (October 2019). Labor Force Characteristics by Race and Ethnicity, 2018. Accessed on March 4, 2020: https://www.bls.gov/opub/reports/race-and-ethnicity/2018/home.htm (Chart 5); Accessed on March 4, 2020: https://www.bls.gov/web/empsit/cpsee_e16.htm

[273] Ibid.

CHAPTER
SIX

A s the saying goes, "give a man a fish, and you feed him for a day. Teach a man to fish, and you feed him for a lifetime."[274] This chapter focuses on mental models and organizational change, two areas critical to making The Big Shift. A 2015 study conducted by the CMO Council found that approximately 67 percent of U.S. marketing executives surveyed said their CMO had high-level support and buy-in for multicultural marketing efforts, but less than one-in-two (45 percent) said their CEO did not believe multicultural consumers were critical to their growth plans.[275] This lack of top-tier support translates into a de-prioritization of multicultural programs across corporate America. The study also found: (1) about half (51 percent) of marketers in the U.S. reported having too many competing priorities within their organizations; (2) only 20 percent of marketers deemed multicultural strategies mandatory and unanimously embraced across their organization, and (3) just over 25 percent believed that multicultural consumers were mission critical for their organization.[276] Are you surprised by these findings?

I'm not. Last year, I set out to better understand if corporate

America was ready for a multicultural America. Our pilot study based on 10 brand marketers across four business categories uncovered key insights that may help explain the CMO Council's findings. The study found that the overwhelming majority (87 percent) of marketing executives in the United States strongly agree/agree that the changing demographic landscape poses a significant challenge to their business.[277] However, 57 percent of marketing executives surveyed strongly agree/agree that multicultural marketing was the responsibility of their ethnic agency, compared to 21 percent who said multicultural marketing was part of their general market agency responsibilities.[278]

What does this all mean? It's reasonable to surmise that marketing executives continue to think about multicultural marketing in a silo (vertical marketing) with Latino, African American and Asian advertising agencies taking the lead in marketing to the ethnic and racial segments. Regardless of their current beliefs, all corporations, sooner than later, will have to revisit their marketing and organizational strategies in a multicultural America, and drive mainstream marketing with multicultural consumers at the core. It's sheer demographics.

In this chapter, I'll examine the relationship between mental models and leadership effectiveness. Chief on the agenda is how mental models are barriers to organizational change, organizational learning and strategic implementation. I'll explore two central questions that impact organizational effectiveness: How and why do mental models pose such a significant management issue to corporate America? And what do these models tell us about the need for The Big Shift?

MENTAL MODELS

Mental models are representations of reality that marketers use to make sense of their world. They're deeply ingrained assumptions that influence how marketers view the business landscape and the actions they take to drive a sustaining competitive advantage. Mental models are developed over time through the process of socialization, which itself is shaped by education, lived experiences and interaction with others. In fact, mental models are so powerful that marketers are not even consciously aware of them or the effect they have on their decision-making process. Mental models often permeate through organizations and across industries by way of repetition, where facts are presented as empirically based and objective, particularly by those who have vested interests in the status quo. Once created, mental models, fixed and ingrained in our minds, are difficult to change.

Because mental models are considered the basic structure of cognition, they're extremely powerful in how they mediate reality and help categorize and organize an endless stream of information. They serve as cognitive structures that attempt to simplify the complex, helping to establish relationships among activities, concepts and abstract items of knowledge. They are cognitive maps or schemas that help guide the understanding of how consumers perceive, decide and act in different environments. Mental models provide a framework for interpreting reality, distinguishing relevance from irrelevance and aiding in the inculcation of new information. For this reason, mental models represent a two-edge sword: They play a role in helping marketers identify opportunities and threats, but they can also stifle creativity and innovation in response to a dynamic environment.

For more than three decades, the advertising and marketing industry perpetuated a mental model around the U.S. Latino consumer that drove colossal growth. The most recent *AdAge Hispanic Fact Pack* puts the Latino ad spend market in excess of $10 billion.[279] As discussed in Chapter 1, the Hispanic Marketing Paradigm was instrumental in shaping the mental model of corporate America around the Latino consumer. Two external forces drew the paradigmatic boundary. The U.S. Census helped quantify the demographic opportunity; in particular, it enumerated the population size and growth rate of Latinos. Second, often in the shadows of the U.S. Census, the Bureau of Labor Statistics (BLS) measured the purchasing power of Latinos and other ethnic groups in the U.S. With these two sources, marketers could make grandiose statements that would catch the attention of every marketer: Latinos are the largest and among the fastest growing segments in the country,[280] with purchasing power exceeding $1.5 trillion annually.[281]

There is an old adage: Demographics is destiny. The population and purchasing power of Latinos and other multicultural segments not only contoured the mental models of corporate America, but it served as the foundation to the Hispanic Marketing Paradigm. It gave birth to an entire new industry — trade associations, advertising agencies, research companies and media publishers. But publishing demographic data wasn't enough to create a sustainable business in marketing to Latinos. It needed to operationalize the consumer and establish new best practices for marketers.

The U.S. Census provided great credibility and a justification in marketing to Latinos. Monetizing the Hispanic Marketing Paradigm required more than descriptive statistics, it required a business strategy. As mentioned earlier in the book, Nielsen began to measure linear television viewership of Latinos, including the Spanish-language duopoly, Univision and Telemundo. To draw investment away from other media properties, in-language publishers developed a sales strategy that positioned all Latinos as culturally different from the mainstream and favored Spanish over English. This was the core of the Paradigm. Reinforced in sales decks, upfront presentations and promotional materials, these principles were cemented into the thinking of corporations and the advertising industry. Corporations, as a result, unequivocally believed that the "best way" to reach Latinos was in Spanish and with in-language media.

One of the principal aims of this book is to dispel any oversimplified mental model around marketing to Latinos and help corporate America make The Big Shift. So far, Chapter 2 presents empirical research challenging the popular monolithic cultural view of Latinos. Chapter 3 debunks the notion that Spanish-language linear television is the single "best way" to reach this entire cohort. Chapter 4 revisits the in-culture marketing approach. Chapter 5 advocates that corporations measure mainstream America by ethnicity and race to better understand the impact of their marketing efforts in a country whose mainstream is no longer comprised of a White majority. And this chapter examines how organizations make decisions. If we want companies to make The Big Shift, we must first address mental models within organizations.

The Hispanic Marketing Paradigm and the mental models associated with it helped differentiate Latinos from other consumers. The stark between-group differences continue to validate a different media approach. And a different marketing strategy. There was a certain logic to creating a business by building a silo to help companies drive growth with Latinos. But as the demographic, technological and media landscapes converged in recent years, marketing in the United States gave rise to new digital companies, new technologies, new customers and new marketing approaches. Latino marketing, meanwhile, doubled down on the Paradigm.[282]

How do corporations make The Big Shift in their mental models? First, leadership within organizations must recognize the need for change and acknowledge that there may be a better way to market their products and services in a multicultural America. This is fundamental to change. Second, organizations stymied by a lack of innovation or adaptation to the marketplace will need to examine the diversity of its leadership or executive team. There is no ideal number or percentage on organizational diversity.[283] To make The Big Shift, corporations must hire and retain for cognitive diversity if they are going to develop mental models that will allow the organization to perceive the world differently.[284] This is precisely one of the reasons why diversity and inclusion are important to the long-term viability of organizations.[285]

Companies can make The Big Shift in two ways, which are not mutually exclusive. Because most corporations in the United States were built in the 20th century, corporations today lack diversity within their organizational structures. The lack of diversity is particularly true in executive boards, the C-suite and senior management inside corporations.[286] One strategy is to hire people who think differently, bring different lived experiences and have different educational backgrounds and skill sets.[287] The other approach, which takes longer to achieve, is to transform the company into a learning organization.[288] This means educating everyone inside the organization on its values, processes and strategies, and requiring that they challenge old mental models with new ones.

Despite the strong link between leadership and mental models, the majority of leadership development focuses on mastering the managerial skills and organizational design necessary to be effective corporate leaders. This is because leaders are generally held responsible for their results and results are attributed to the actions of leaders. In addition, most leadership and organizational development programs address a number of activities that are ancillary to challenging one's mental models. Although having skills in organization development are helpful, they aren't sufficient for leadership effectiveness. Exceptional leadership requires that leaders challenge their mental models, assumptions, beliefs and values that feed their decision-making processes. Exceptional leaders have a high EQ and a strong understanding that their worldview bears far more influence on corporate outcomes than their decisions or actions.

How companies see their world affects how they perceive their competitors as well as the actions their organizations take to exploit business opportunities. When leaders challenge and change their mental models, they can then – and only then – change their actions and expect very different results. Unlike reacting, which occurs when marketers respond to a new condition by doing what they've always done, leaders should respond to change by questioning their mental models. In this process called reframing, their deeply held assumptions and governing principles come under scrutiny. Only after leaders know and question their underlying assumptions can they open themselves to new ways of seeing and thinking.

MENTAL MODELS AS BARRIERS TO CHANGE

Corporations were founded on concepts from 17th-century Newtonian physics, which assume the world is stable, linear and predictable. The thought is that fixed structures provide stability, clarity and order; but the fact is, they typically function only within the finite contexts for which they were designed. When new conditions arise, like a global financial crisis or the recent COVID-19 pandemic, corporations often fail in their response because they are unable to adapt to the volatile environment and its novel complexities. They frequently see solutions to their problems limited by resources – such as time, people or money.

The concept of mental models is not new. The term mental model was first introduced in *The Nature of Explanations* by Scottish psychologist Kenneth Craik, who believed that the mind constructs small-scale models of reality that are used to anticipate events, reason and undergird explanation. In ancient history, the Greek philosopher Plato tells an allegory of the cave in his well-known dialogue *Republic*, in which he concludes that we're all misguided cave dwellers, operating under incomplete or distorted perceptions of reality. The point of the story is that humans are very resistant to rethinking and transforming their own perceptions of reality. What Plato was suggesting is that due to our mental models, people find change difficult.

Mental models function as filters that allow only a limited portion of the external stimuli to enter our brain. This process is useful for triaging input to prevent information overload, but the problem is that organizational stakeholders generally have a tendency to reject data that doesn't support an already existing assumption. What's unfamiliar or incongruent to their worldview is quickly discarded as irrelevant or unimportant. As they try to comprehend their environment through categories that worked for them in the past, the trouble sets in. For this reason, mental models are often the greatest barriers to implementing new ideas or approaches within organizations.

In fact, new ideas often die on the vine because they simply don't match the prevailing ideology, assumptions and beliefs. Companies that are not afraid to introduce new models of thinking tend to adapt to the changing environment better than companies whose mental models act as buffers in their organizations. Mental models in some ways are equivalent to the concept of a paradigm because a paradigm and mental models represent an integrative set of ideas and practices that shape the way employees and companies, ultimately, view and interact with the world.

Managers tend to have a fixed mindset in part because they tend to filter out information that doesn't fit their current paradigm. In order to avoid this, managers must question the old paradigm and step outside their preconceived mental models to keep pace with an ever-changing environment. By challenging the paradigm, managers must re-imagine new ways to understand the future that doesn't logically follow from its past. If mental models are left unchallenged, they cause managers to see what they have always seen: the same results, the same issues, the same opportunities. Because we tend to see what our mental models allow us to see, we can only do what our mental models permit us to do. For this reason, managers must first identify what their internal assumptions are, and then unlearn what they think they know.

MENTAL MODELS AS ORGANIZATIONAL LEARNING BARRIERS

Management in the 21st century is about what we might call change learning. As technology and information continue to reshape our world and subsequently corporations, managers are becoming change agents who guide employees to find and embrace new practices. Every employee must be a learner, and the manager's foremost task is to promote learning. As stated by Peter Senge, a learning organization is an organization where people continually expand their capacity to create the results they truly desire, where new and expansive patterns of thinking are nurtured, where collective aspiration is set free, and where people are continually learning how to learn together.[289]

A learning organization represents a great tool for managers because it helps employees learn more about the products and processes within their organizations and others in order to remain competitive and answer challenges in today's fast-changing business environment. Since the greatest constant of modern times is change, companies today must learn faster than their competitors in order to stay ahead of the game. A learning organization becomes imperative because it enables employees to continuously share and obtain new knowledge while applying their newfound knowledge in doing their work or in making organizational decisions.

Since mental models represent the assumptions held by people who determine how an organization thinks and acts, employees are a significant barrier for organizational learning. Mental models can affect decision making and implementing strategic orientation and can damage overall organizational development. It's important to distinguish between what Senge calls espoused theories and theories-in-use. Espoused theory relates to "what we say we do," whereas theory-in-use is "what we actually do" based on our own mental models. Leaders should facilitate this practice by regularly asking company members about what's working and what's not. A company that enforces such conversations is a learning organization because they've embraced the idea that being a learning organization is a good thing, so learning becomes a mental model in itself. Another important part of reflective conversations for organizational learning is the role of teams. Senge finds that teams, not individuals, are the fundamental learning unit in modern organizations.[290] He emphasizes that the dialogue among the members of the team increases the organization's ability organization to grow and develop.

It's not enough to hire great people. Senge identifies three conditions that are necessary for dialogue: (1) participants must suspend their assumptions, (2) they must regard one another as colleagues, and (3) there must be a facilitator to hold the context of the dialogue (a facilitator is needed at least until teams develop dialogue skills).[291] The democratizing thrust is essential for productive results, given that hierarchy is both antithetical to dialogue – and difficult to escape in organizations.[292] Organizational structure ultimately is a driving factor in organizational excellence.

It bears noting that hierarchy and patterns of relationships are also derived from people's mental models. Capitalizing on the synergy of group learning for optimal performance, organizational learning requires that individuals in the organization must be ready and willing to reveal their own mental models, compare them to others' and discuss the differences in order to come to a unified perception of what really is. Leadership is a process grounded in relationships that are fluid, non-directional and non-unilateral.[293] This is a fundamental shift away from a paradigm that has historically centralized leadership at the individual level – a shift that spreads the power of leadership across people and teams within an organization.

According to Etienne Wenger, a social researcher and champion of communities of practice, learning is best envisioned as an interaction among peers, rather than as a vertical transmission of knowledge.[294] Organizations are not responsible for employee learning. Just the opposite. Employees and managers are there to help organizations learn more effectively.[295] The organization must ensure that the strategies and conditions exist so people can continuously learn. Such arrangements reflect the assumption that people feel secure about offering information — good or bad, or consistent or not with the organization's prevailing worldview. This means that organizations must be transformed into places where it's safe to reveal new knowledge that may be disruptive. When this happens, managers can go about their real business, which is managing a company's knowledge through its people.

In the context of organizational learning, management becomes an art of managing knowledge. In other words, what's being managed are not people, per se, but rather the knowledge they carry. Good leadership means creating the conditions that enable people to produce valid knowledge and in ways that encourage personal responsibility. Focusing on knowledge management in organizations, Chris Argyris's seminal book *Knowledge for Action* talks about two types of organizations, Model I and Model II organizations.[296] Argyris explains how, based on the prevailing type of mental model, organizations are managing either valid or invalid knowledge. According to Argyris, mental models manifest in the organization's ability to perform and compete.

Model I organizations have institutionalized a form of self-censorship that is defensive, limiting open communication.[297] If employees believe that sharing bad news at the meeting is going to upset management, they will refrain. As a result, organizations tend to cultivate invalid knowledge about their current business and overall reality.[298] So when this type of organization is in trouble, which Argyris suggests that is the case with the majority of organizations in the U.S., employees are so distanced from their own reality that they are unable to see or clearly understand organizational problems. This is because: Although people do not always behave congruently with what they say (espoused theories), they do behave congruently with their mental models (theories in use).[299]

Model II companies have a better way of communicating because they deal with so-called valid knowledge.[300] This enables them to assess reality more correctly and consequently solve problems more effectively because the prevailing ideology created a culture that reinforces organizational learning. This ability is crucial for the survival of an organization in a highly complex and constantly changing business environment.[301]

MENTAL MODELS AS BARRIERS TO STRATEGIC IMPLEMENTATION

Mental models limit organizations every day. According to Kohl's article on strategic park planning failure, many implementation barriers grow out of managers' assumptions or mental models.[302] What many organizations call planning is simply a projection of their current mental models into the future. Planning also tends to fail within organizations because planning assumptions are often invalid. In order to avoid this, the planning process must, to some extent, expose and challenge the organization's mental models. This does not mean that all mental models should be changed during the planning process, but some will have to change before correcting course for the future. The most common misstep is a failure to rethink or reframe the problem (especially among employees), which leaves the underlying pattern of thought unchanged. For this reason, resources and time in today's organizations are mostly spent on reorganizing structures and procedures and reacting on issues. Many innovative ideas never develop into meaningful decisions or ladder up to a key strategy in organizations because they are not congruent with the company's dominant mental models.

Systems thinking, however, views an organization not as a

group of separate parts but as a complex system with multiple feedbacks and delays. As such, leaders in organizations must have the capacity to identify and examine their assumptions or mental models. Only when these assumptions are identified and tested can organizations continuously adapt and improve. Once the mind is shut off to new ways, assumptions grow hard and immobile, and a changing context will pass them by. According to Chris Argyris, there are two simple but powerful mechanisms that block our mental models.[303] The first is called defensive routines, which are policies or actions that are put in place to prevent workers and organizations from experiencing embarrassment or threat.[304] Defensive routines are anti-learning and overprotective and they are a main obstacle from having an open mind. Argyris also talks about skilled incompetence.[305] Skilled because we do it without thinking (like riding a bike), and incompetence because it creates results that are not intended (like falling from a bike). In practice, this occurs when the environment changes and employees continue to behave according to the same mental model. Managers use practiced routine behaviors (skill) to produce what they do not intend (incompetence). Similarly, an organization may suffer negative or disastrous consequences of skilled incompetence. The only remedy is to find out how deeply ingrained the incompetence is and to unlearn it.

CONCLUSION AND IMPLICATIONS

Leadership effectiveness is strongly associated with the ability to learn and change mental models. Only after uncovering their internal assumptions can marketers create a future that's different from their past. According to Peter Senge, managing mental models involves identifying, clarifying and changing one's mental model and its component assumptions. It's only through such a process of deconstruction that mental models can be challenged, enabling marketers to identify new ways of looking at an old problem differently. The current socio-political and economic climate requires a new approach that requires leaders to think differently about how change occurs and how professionals develop themselves and work with each other. For example, how can a manager deal effectively with an interpersonal problem in their unit if they have certain opinions about an individual? To be an effective leader requires the discipline of mental models, which means being able to modify assumptions in order to show the true causes of problems.

The fact is that leaders today frequently face challenges and opportunities that cannot be adequately addressed by reflecting on the past. Organizational leaders must be able to overcome the limitations of their own mental models to develop a new understanding that will ensure the development of innovative and effective strategies to deal with a new reality. In his book *Community: The Structure of Belonging*, Peter Block suggests that a paradigm shift in management is needed to focus on what companies can create, rather than on what problems they can solve. From Block's perspective, in order to nurture the possibility of a future different from the past, marketers must move away from low-hanging fruit and cultivate more sustainable solutions rooted in meaningful questioning and engagement. Only through such transformative participation can our fragmented worldview be replaced with an integrated whole systems mental model. Because learning involves a movement of the mind, the primary task of leaders today is to be learners themselves and to promote and facilitate learning so that people can continually expand their capabilities to clarify their vision, understand complexity and improve shared mental models within their teams and across the organization. Only then can corporations begin to make The Big Shift.

CHAPTER SIX ENDNOTES

[274] Although the origin of this thought has been debated, it has been attributed to 12th century philosopher Maimonides.

[275] The CMO Council. (2015). Activating the New American Mainstream. Defining, Reaching and Engaging the Multicultural Market. Accessed on https://www.cmocouncil.org/thought-leadership/reports/activating-the-new-american-mainstream

[276] Ibid.

[277] Beniflah, J. (2020). Is Corporate America Ready for a Multicultural America? Unpublished Pilot Study.

[278] Ibid.

[279] Hispanic Fact Pack. (2019). *AdAge*. New York: Crain Communications, Inc.

[280] U.S. Census Bureau, 2020.

[281] Humphreys, J. (2018). The Multicultural Economy 2019. The Selig Center. Atlanta: The University of Georgia.

[282] Ayala, J. (2019). Univision "Reaches for the Heart" During 2019-20 Upfronts. MediaVillage. Accessed on July 9, 2020: https://www.mediavillage.com/article/univision-reaches-for-the-heart-during-2019-20-upfronts/

[283] Reddy, S. and Jadhav, A. (2019). Gender diversity in boardrooms – A literature review. *Cogent Economics & Finance*. 7:1-11.

[284] Page, S. (2007). The Difference: How the Power of Diversity Creates Better Groups, Firms, Schools, and Societies - New Edition. Princeton: Princeton University Press.

[285] Ibid.

[286] Reddy, S. and Jadhav, A. (2019). Gender diversity in boardrooms – A literature review. *Cogent Economics & Finance*. 7:1-11.

[287] Ibid.

[288] Senge, P. (1990). The Fifth Discipline: The Art and Practice of the Learning Organization. New York: Currency Doubleday

[289] Ibid.

[290] Ibid.

[291] Ibid.

[292] Ibid.

[293] Ibid.

[294] Ibid.

[295] Wenger, E. (1998). Communities of Practice: Learning, Meaning, And Identity (Learning in Doing: Social, Cognitive and Computational Perspectives). Cambridge: Cambridge University Press.

[296] Argyris, C. (1993). Knowledge for Action: A Guide to Overcoming Barriers to Organizational Change. San Francisco: Jossey-Bass, Inc.

[297] Ibid.

[298] Ibid.

[299] Ibid.

[300] Ibid.

[301] Ibid.

[302] Kohl, J. (2006). Mental Models That Block Strategic Plan Implementation. *Reflections*. 7(1): 30-42.

[303] Argyris, C. and Schön, D. (1996). Organizational Learning II: Theory, Methods and Practice. Boston: Addison-Wesley.

[304] Ibid.

[305] Ibid.

CHAPTER
SEVEN

Marketing effectiveness is a two-sided coin. Marketing is built around identifying consumer insights and developing powerful communication strategies. Being effective deals with creating organizational capabilities to drive a sustaining a competitive advantage. Over the course of my career, I have learned it is much easier to change consumer behavior than it is to transform an organization. Corporations built in the 20th century will die if they do not adapt to the changing environment. The challenge in prescribing a fixed set of solutions, however, is that all corporations do not share the same institutional knowledge or face similar competitive threats, making a one-size-fits-all strategy difficult to remedy all of corporate America's ailments.

In this chapter, I propose a number of key success factors that will help companies sustain growth. I discuss the so-called "paradox" in building core competencies and ends with a practical marketing framework proven to drive firm performance. Successful companies in the 21st century will need to develop a set of dynamic capabilities to address an ever-changing demographic and business landscape. As such, the purpose of this chapter is to help corporate America get ready for a multicultural America.

ORGANIZATIONAL CAPABILITIES

Based on the Resource-Based View, organizational capabilities are considered a major source in generating and developing a sustainable competitive advantage.[306] [307] Markets in which firms compete for pre-eminence must build capabilities that are heterogeneous across their competitive terrain. By leveraging these differences, organizations build a competitive advantage to drive and sustain long-term growth.[308-310] A firm's strategic position, as a result, can vary significantly based on the availability and allocation of resources that are unique and relatively superior to other organizations. The central notion of developing a sustainable competitive edge is for an organization to create more value than the least efficient competitor.[311]

For those interested in understanding its origins, building organizational capabilities has been based on evolutionary economics.[312-314] Capabilities are developed in the context of organizational resource allocation, which is embedded in idiosyncratic social structures. On this basis, capabilities are conceived as distinct behavioral patterns. These are not only complex in nature and involve formal and informal processes[315-317] but representative of a repository of historical experiences and organizational learning.[318] It is the compilation and integration of these building blocks that serve as the foundation of a sustainable competitive advantage.

Although organizational capabilities have been vaguely defined,[319] they are referred to in a number of ways: core competencies,[320] collective skills,[321] complex routines,[322] critical success factors and best practices. These capabilities do not represent a single resource, but rather a distinctive way in which companies allocate their internal and external resources. At play are complex processes across different functions of an organization that can make its value proposition nearly non-imitable and unique to that firm. In contrast to rational choice theory, whose focus is on single actor decisions, organizational capabilities are seen as collective and socially embedded in nature. They are brought about by social interactions and represent problem solving in a collective manner that is driven by people and organizational processes.[323]

In developing organizational capabilities in highly volatile markets, the reliance on a specific set of nurtured capabilities has been called into question. Instead, the emphasis must shift to a company's ability to change and quickly generate new capabilities as a prerequisite of a sustained competitive advantage. The salient concepts in this debate are "dynamic capabilities" [324-328] and "dynamic core competencies," [329 330] both of which call for a profound dynamization of organizational capabilities.

The notion of "dynamic" is central to creating the continuous renewal of organizational capabilities, thereby matching the demands of a rapidly changing environment. As such, the concept of dynamic capabilities upends the Resource-Based View, insofar as how fluid and flexible a company's organizational capabilities need to be in response to the unfolding business environment.[331] Dynamic capabilities must meet three important threshold requirements: problem solving and complexity; practicing and success; and reliability and time.

PROBLEM SOLVING AND COMPLEXITY

Capabilities are conceptualized in the context of collective organizational problem solving. Capable firms are assumed to solve emerging problems effectively. A capability is not attributed, however, unless outstanding skills have solved extraordinary problems. The notion of complexity refers to the characteristics of problems and decision-making under uncertainty,[332] [333] addressing ambiguous, ill structured tasks.[334] [335] Solving complex tasks requires sophisticated abilities with a broad absorptive capacity, which refers to a company's ability to recognize the value of new information, assimilate it and apply it to commercial ends.[336] [337] As is well known from cybernetics, complexity needs complexity.[338] The complexity of a capability reflects the internal requirements for mastering complex tasks.

Problem solving can be defined as a sequence of generating complex combinations of cognitive and habitual acts.[339] These acts focus primarily on finding all the relevant resources needed and combining them effectively.[340] Due to its complexity, the organization may effectively solve challenging problems without understanding the inherent logic of its capability; its internal functioning is likely to remain opaque. Organizational capabilities are not the result of planned corporate conduct. They emerge incrementally from daily interaction and are often considered mysterious social phenomena.[341]

PRACTICING AND SUCCESS

Capabilities are closely related to action. Embedding organizational capabilities into an organization's practices means that a capability represents more than explicit knowledge. Capabilities are fundamentally embedded in emotions, mental models and tacit knowledge.[342] [343] Practicing a capability has been referred to as a "generative dance" between explicit and tacit elements.[344]

Capabilities are also bound to performance; they are conceived as actions that are recognized and valued within an organization.[345] [346] However, they are only recognized as and attributed to organizational performance when they drive success relative to its nearest competitor. Finally, and most importantly, a single case of mastering a problem situation does not amount to an organizational capability. The notion of capabilities refers to habitualized action patterns or routines, which some researchers refer to as the building blocks of organizational capabilities.[347-349]

RELIABILITY AND TIME

In order for something to qualify as a capability, it must work in a reliable manner.[350] A set of problem-solving activities is not called a capability unless it has been proven to be successful across various situations and organizations. As a consequence, for an organization, the ability to transform an accidentally successful coordination effort into a reliable problem-solving pattern is of critical importance.[351] [352] A singular success can trigger the building of a capability, but a capability is not actually constituted unless a reliable practice has evolved over time. An organizational capability, in fact, is a historical concept by its very nature, integrating past experiences with the present problem-solving activities and a prospect for future direction of resource allocation.

Stressing the historical nature of organizational capabilities suggests that time is a basic dimension of capabilities. Capability development comes close to a chain of reactions triggered by an initial event, thereby establishing a capability trajectory. Capability development takes time, and the specific way in which time is spent (i.e., the intensity, frequency and duration of social interactions) is relevant for the creation of a capability. At the same time, the particular importance of this process means that there are no time compression economies.[353] It should be reiterated that it is exactly this time-intensive dimension that makes up the inimitable essence of organizational capabilities.[354] [355] Time gives organizations the ability to develop capabilities that not only are unique but provide a competitive advantage.

Overall, any organizational capability is the result of an organizational learning process in which a specific way of selecting and linking resources gradually develops. Although organizational capabilities apply to various problem situations, they do not necessarily apply to all problems. Sometimes they are formed through successful responses to specific historical challenges and are therefore bound to specific types of problems.[356] Problem solving is inherent in organizational design, information procedures, micropolitics and communication channels, among other organizational elements. All of these elements shape organizational capabilities and thus define their unique distinctiveness.[357]

THE PARADOX IN ORGANIZATIONAL CAPABILITIES

Developing organizational capabilities is a prerequisite for market success. But that success often times comes with a heavy price, particularly for firms that are in highly volatile markets or where technology and subsequently consumer behavior is rapidly changing. Needless to say, capabilities are considered core if they differentiate a company strategically. Core capabilities evolve, and a company's survival depends on their ability to successfully manage that evolution. However, organizations face an interesting and unexpecting paradox: Core capabilities simultaneously enhance and inhibit development. In other words, core competencies can lead to core rigidities.[358] The fundamental issue is that organizations are unable to change their familiar ways of doing when confronted with new developments in their external environments. This inherent tendency toward inertia is one of the reasons why companies must develop and foster capabilities that are dynamic. This paradox is rooted in a number of factors. I outline three of them: (1) path dependence, (2) structural inertia and (3) organizational commitment.

PATH DEPENDENCE

Organizations are often overly persistent in their strategic orientation, which has been explained by a phenomenon called path dependence. This concept refers to a company's current and future decision capabilities that are imprinted by past decisions and their underlying patterns.[359] [360] In many cases, path dependence means more than mere historical imprinting. It refers to forceful dynamics that help drive increasing returns.[361] Successful combinatorial activities generate positive feedback loops that serve as self-reinforcing processes. These processes may establish strategic paths that are prone to narrowing the scope of strategic management.[362-364] Often, a specific orientation becomes locked within an organization, and all strategic alternatives are subsequently ignored. The same is true for capability building where positive feedback processes are likely to bring about path dependence. Organizational capabilities are prone to becoming fixed to strategies that have proven to be successful in an organization's past, which limits a company's desire or ability to explore new strategies that may be better suited for a different future.

STRUCTURAL INERTIA

Organizational inertia is a precondition for organizational success.[365] Inertia is needed to make an organization reliable and identifiable as a distinct unit. It is, in fact, a requirement for guaranteed survival. But, paradoxically, inertia brings about the risk of maladaptation. In the face of a changing environment, organizations are bound to their stabilized structures. Central to survival, in the end, is for an organization to overcome organizational inertia.

Other approaches locate organizational inertia primarily in other mechanisms such as change-inhibiting organizational cultures.[366] Another stream of research addresses the capability paradox in the context of organizational learning.[367] The basic idea is that focusing on improving existing capabilities makes experimentation with alternatives less attractive.[368-371] By exploiting current strengths, there is a tendency to crowd out explorative activities that go beyond the beaten track. As organizations develop greater competence in a particular activity, they engage in that activity more, thus further increasing competence and the opportunity cost of exploration.[372] These exploitation processes not only lead to a fixation on existing capabilities, but also prevent developing new capabilities.[373] Thus, capability development resides in the well-known trade-off between exploitation and exploration processes in organizational learning.[374]

ORGANIZATIONAL COMMITMENT

Further insight into the nature of the capability paradox is based on the commitment of an organization, which highlights the binding effects of investments and the resulting persistence of organizational strategies.[375] Commitment to a particular strategy is considered the prerequisite for sustained competitive advantage. Firm-specific investments are needed to build heterogeneity and superior performance.[376] However, investments in firm-specific resources are likely to be irreversible and rigid because the cost of separating and abandoning such sticky resources is too high. The consequence is that resource commitment tends to restrict an organization's options and flexibility.[377] The more dynamic the environment, the higher the implied flexibility risk.[378] Capabilities do not actually represent a specific single resource; they become the combination and linking of resources.

Resources and capabilities represent two different conceptual levels with their own dynamics. The commitment to resources resulting from specific investments should be clearly differentiated from commitments evolving when practicing capabilities. This differentiation implies a separation of resource-based inertia and capability-based rigidity.[379] In the end, organizations seeking a sustained competitive advantage will need to be committed toward building a set of capabilities but remain flexible enough to change their commitments given the changing external environments.

EMPIRICAL FRAMEWORK

The following part of this chapter introduces a framework that can help organizations drive a competitive advantage in a multicultural America. It is an empirical model that I have adapted to help corporations in any business category develop dynamic capabilities.[380] The proposed framework is prescriptive, helping organizations develop the right type of marketing capabilities and market orientation to align with a changing environment. This model can be used as a benchmark to measure a company's dynamic capabilities over time.

MARKET ORIENTATION

Let me begin by reviewing the theoretical underpinning of the proposed framework. Dynamic Capability Theory posits that organizational performance is a by-product when specific resources are acquired and deployed as capabilities in order to match the firm's dynamic market environment.[381-383] Over time, these capabilities involve complex coordinated patterns of skills and knowledge that become inscribed as organizational routines[384] and are distinguished from other organizational processes by performing better than its rivals.[385][386] Capabilities are dynamic when they enable a firm to implement new strategies to reflect changing market conditions by combining and transforming available resources in new and different ways.[387]

In addition, research indicates that while possessing valuable, rare, inimitable and non-substitutable resources may be beneficial, organizations also require complementary capabilities to be able to deploy available resources in ways that match the market conditions to drive firm performance.[388] [389] Market orientation is the extent to which a company engages in the generation, dissemination and response to market intelligence pertaining to current and future customer needs, competitor strategies and actions, channel requirements and abilities and to the broader business environment.[390]

Drawing on the traditional Resource-Based View, research suggests that firms with superior market orientation achieve superior business performance because they have a greater understanding of customers' expressed wants and hidden needs, competitor capabilities and strategies, channel requirements and developments and the broader market environment than their rivals.[391] [392] This represents a "know-what" advantage that enables the firm to be both more effective and efficient by allowing managers to select the most productive available resource combinations to match market conditions.[393]

MARKETING CAPABILITIES

Considerably less attention has been paid to the capabilities by which firms deploy their market orientation into target markets. Capabilities may be viewed at different levels in the firm, many of which cross different functional areas.[394] However, capabilities relating to market resource deployment are usually associated with the marketing function.[395] [396] As depicted in Figure 7, there are two interrelated marketing capability areas: capabilities concerning individual marketing mix processes, such as product development and management, pricing, selling, marketing communications and channel management[397] and capabilities concerned with the processes of marketing strategy development and execution.[398] [399] These capabilities may be rare, valuable, non-substitutable and inimitable sources of advantage that can lead to superior firm performance.[400] [401] As knowledge-based processes become embedded over time, these capabilities become difficult for competitors to imitate.[402]

THE INTERACTION EFFECT

Both the Resource-Based View and its Dynamic Capability extensions reinforce the importance of the interaction between a firm's "know-what" knowledge resources and its complementary "know-how" deployment capabilities.[403] This suggests that a firm's market orientation and marketing capabilities may interact to align its resources with its market environment better than its rivals.[404] [405]

There are two main reasons to expect such an interaction. First, resource-based theory indicates that deployment capabilities offer economies of scale in their knowledge resources.[406] [407] Marketing capabilities are viewed as important market-relating mechanisms by which superior market knowledge may be deployed by companies to generate profits,[408] [409] making them particularly complementary with firms' market orientation.[410]

Second, as market orientation and marketing capabilities are complementary to one another in ways that generate superior economic value, and each may be viewed as an individual source of competitive advantage, the interaction between market orientation and marketing capabilities possesses the characteristic of asset inter-connectedness.[411] This creates causal ambiguity that makes it particularly difficult for competitors to disentangle the source of a firm's observed performance advantage.[412] It also requires that a rival company acquire both the interconnected market orientation and marketing capabilities of a high-performing firm that bases its strategy on these co-specialized assets to be able to compete away its performance advantage.[413-415]

CONCLUSION

Leaders in major corporations are likely to spend years building their best practices with the plan of deploying resources that provide their organization with a sustaining competitive advantage.[416] In this chapter, I discuss the paradox that exists in building core competencies. Corporations in high volatile markets are likely to experience diminishing returns from their core competencies given that they no longer help the organization navigate the dynamic landscape effectively.

There is research to support the Resource-Based View in directly linking market orientation with firm performance.[417] Consistent with the Resource-Based View and Dynamic Capabilities Theory, which propose that the differences in performance between firms can be explained by the heterogeneity in organizational capabilities, research has shown that there is a significant direct relationship between firms' marketing capabilities and organizational performance.[418] While the notion that market-relating capabilities are key to understanding firm performance,[419] it has received little empirical interest,[420] and even less attention on the types of market-relating capabilities that are needed in a changing multicultural America. Rather than provide a one-size-fits-all, pre-fixed solution, I believe companies will fare better if they develop unique dynamic capabilities that effectively address *their* changing demographic and business landscapes.[421] [422] The proposed model outlined in this chapter can serve as one framework that will better prepare corporate America for a multicultural America.

Figure 7
Empirical Framework

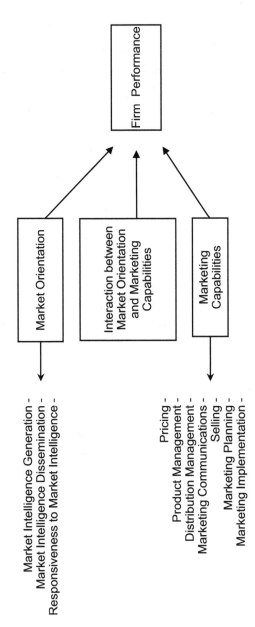

Adapted from: Morgan, N., Vorhies, D., and Mason, C. (2009). Marketing Orientation, Marketing Capabilities and Firm Performance. *Strategic Management Journal.* 30: 909-920.

CHAPTER SEVEN ENDNOTES

[306] Barney, J. (1991). Firm Resources and Sustained Competitive Advantage. *Journal of Management.* 17(1): 99-120.

[307] Wernerfelt, B. (1984). A Resource-Based View of the Firm. *Strategic Management Journal.* 5(2): 171-180.

[308] Amit, R. and Schoemaker, P. (1993). Strategic Assets and Organizational Rent. *Strategic Management Journal.* 14(1): 33-46.

[309] Barney J. (1997). Looking Inside for Competitive Advantage. In Core Competency-Based Strategy. Campbell A, Sommers LK (eds). London: International Thomson Business Press, 13-29.

[310] Peteraf, M. (1993). The Cornerstones of Competitive Advantage: A Resource-Based View. *Strategic Management Journal.* 14(3): 179-191.

[311] Peteraf, M. and Barney, J. (2003). Unraveling the Resource-Based Tangle. *Managerial and Decision Economics.* 24(1): 309-323.

[312] Helfat C. and Peteraf, M. (2003). The Dynamic Resource-Based View: Capability Lifecycles. *Strategic Management Journal.* 24(10): 997-1010.

[313] Nelson, R. and Winter, S. (1982). An Evolutionary Theory of Economic Change. Cambridge: Belknap Press of Harvard University Press.

[314] Winter, S. (2003). Understanding Dynamic Capabilities. *Strategic Management Journal.* 24(10): 991-995.

[315] Dosi, G., Nelson, R., and Winter, S. (2000). Introduction: The Nature and Dynamics of Organizational Capabilities. In the Nature and Dynamics of Organizational Capabilities, Dosi, G., and Nelson. R., Winter S. (eds). New York: Oxford University Press, 1-22.

[316] Hofer, C. and Schendel, D. (1978). Strategy Formulation: Analytical Concepts. St Paul: West.

[317] Sanchez, R. and Mahoney, J. (1996). Modularity, Flexibility, and Knowledge Management in Product and Organization Design. *Strategic Management Journal.* Winter Special Issue, 17: 63-76.

[318] Winter, S. (2000). The Satisficing Principle in Capability Learning. *Strategic Management Journal.* Special Issue. 21(10-11): 981-996.

[319] Collis, D. (1994). Research Note: How Valuable Are Organizational Capabilities. *Strategic Management Journal.* 15(8): 143-152.

[320] Javidan, M. (1998). Core competence: What Does It Mean in Practice? *Long Range Planning.* February. 31(1): 60-71.

[321] Sawang, S., Parker, R., and Hine, D. (2016). How Small Business Advisory Program Delivery Methods (Collective Learning, Tailored and

Practice-Based Approaches) Affect Learning and Innovation. *Journal of Small Business Management.* 54(1): 244-261.

[322] Akgün, A., Byrne, J., Lynn, G., and Keskin, H. (2007). Organizational Unlearning as Changes in Beliefs and Routines in Organizations. *The Journal of Organizational Change Management.* 20(6): 794-812.

[323] Cyert, R. and March, J. (1963). A Behavioral Theory of the Firm. Englewood Cliffs: Prentice-Hall.

[324] Teece, D., Pisano, G., and Shuen, A. (1997). Dynamic Capabilities and Strategic Management. *Strategic Management Journal.* 18(7): 509-535.

[325] Kusunoki, K., Nonaka, I., and Nagata, A. (1998). Organizational Capabilities in Product Development of Japanese Firms: A Conceptual Framework and Empirical Findings. *Organization Science.* 9(6): 699-718.

[326] Eisenhardt, M. and Martin, J. (2000). Dynamic Capabilities: What Are They? *Strategic Management Journal.* Oct-Nov, Special Issue. 21: 1105-1121.

[327] Zollo, M. and Winter, S. (2002). Deliberate Learning and The Evolution of Dynamic Capabilities. *Organization Science.* 13(3): 339-351.

[328] Winter, S. (2003). Understanding Dynamic Capabilities. *Strategic Management Journal.* 24(10): 991-995.

[329] Danneels, E. (2002). The Dynamics of Product Innovation and Firm Competencies. *Strategic Management Journal.* 23(12): 1095-1121.

[330] Lei, D., Hitt, M., and Bettis, R. (1996). Dynamic Core Competencies Through Meta-Learning and Strategic Context. *Journal of Management.* 22(4): 549-569.

[331] Helfat C. and Peteraf, M. (2003). The Dynamic Resource-Based View: Capability Lifecycles. *Strategic Management Journal.* 24(10): 997-1010.

[332] Dosi, G., Hobday, M., and Marengo, L. (2003). Problem-solving behavior, organizational forms, and the complexity of tasks. In the SMS Blackwell Handbook of Organizational Capabilities, CE Helfat (ed). Malden: Blackwell, 167-192.

[333] Duncan, R. (1972). Characteristics of organizational environments and perceived environmental uncertainty. *Administrative Science Quarterly.* 17: 313-328.

[334] March J. and Olsen J. (1976). Ambiguity and Choice in Organization. Bergen: Universitetsforlaget.

[335] March, J. and Simon, H. (1958). Organizations. New York: Wiley.

[336] Cohen, W. and Levinthal D. (1990). Absorptive capacity: a new perspective on learning and innovation. *Administrative Sciences Quarterly.* 35(1): 128-152.

[337] Zahra, S. and George, G. (2002). Absorptive capacity: a review, reconceptualization, and extension. *Academy of Management Review.* 27: 185–203.

[338] Ashby, W. (1965). An Introduction to Cybernetics. London: Methuen.

[339] Dosi, G., Nelson, R., and Winter, S. (2000). Introduction: The Nature and Dynamics of Organizational Capabilities. In the Nature and Dynamics of Organizational Capabilities, Dosi, G., Nelson, R., Winter, S. (eds). New York: Oxford University Press, 1-22.

[340] Kogut, B. and Zander, U. (1992). Knowledge of the firm, Combinative Capabilities, and the Replication of Technology. *Organization Science.* 3: 383-397.

[341] Dosi, G., Nelson, R., and Winter, S. (2000). Introduction: The Nature and Dynamics of Organizational Capabilities. In the Nature and Dynamics of Organizational Capabilities, Dosi, G., Nelson, R., Winter, S. (eds). New York: Oxford University Press, 1-22.

[342] Polanyi, M. (1958). Personal Knowledge. Chicago: University of Chicago Press.

[343] Polanyi, M. (1966). The Tacit Dimension. London: Routledge & Kegan Paul.

[344] Cook, S. and Brown J. (1999). Bridging Epistemologies: The Generative Dance Between Organizational Knowledge and Organizational Knowing. *Organization Science.* 10(4): 382- 400.

[345] Gherardi, S. and Nicolini, D. (2002). Learning in a Constellation of Interconnected Practices: Canon or Dissonance? *Journal of Management Studies.* 39(4): 419-436.

[346] Weinert, F. (2001). Concept of Competence: A Conceptual Clarification. In Defining and Selecting Key Competencies, Rychen DS, Salganik LH (eds). Seattle: Hogrefe & Huber, 45-65.

[347] Dosi, G., Nelson, R., and Winter, S. (2000). Introduction: The Nature and Dynamics of Organizational Capabilities. In the Nature and Dynamics of Organizational Capabilities, Dosi, G., Nelson, R., Winter, S. (eds). New York: Oxford University Press, 1-22.

[348] Nelson, R. and Winter, S. (1982). An Evolutionary Theory of Economic Change. Cambridge: Belknap Press of Harvard University Press.

[349] Winter S. (2000). The Satisficing Principle in Capability Learning. *Strategic Management Journal.* Special Issue. 21(10–11): 981-996.

[350] Helfat C. and Peteraf, M. (2003). The Dynamic Resource-Based View: Capability Lifecycles. *Strategic Management Journal.* 24(10): 997-1010.

[351] Hannan, M. and Freeman, J. (1977). The Population Ecology of Organizations. *American Journal of Sociology*. 82: 929-964.

[352] Hannan, M. and Freeman J. (1984). Structural Inertia and Organizational Change. *American Sociological Review*. 49: 149-164.

[353] Dierickx, I. and Cool, K. (1989). Asset Stock Accumulation and Sustainability of Competitive Advantage. *Management Science*. 3: 1504-1510.

[354] Barney, J. (1991). Firm Resources and Sustained Competitive Advantage. *Journal of Management*. 17(1): 99-120.

[355] Leonard-Barton, D. (1992). Core Capabilities and Core Rigidities: A Paradox in Managing New Product Development. *Strategic Management Journal*: 13(5): 111-126.

[356] Winter, S. (2003). Understanding Dynamic Capabilities. *Strategic Management Journal*: 24(10): 991-995.

[357] Henderson, R. and Clark, K. (1990). Architectural Innovation: The Reconfiguration of Existing Product Technologies and the Failure of Established Firms. *Administrative Science Quarterly*. 35(1): 9-30.

[358] Leonard-Barton, D. (1992). Core Capabilities and Core Rigidities: A Paradox in Managing New Product Development. *Strategic Management Journal*. Special Issue: Strategy Process: Managing Corporate Self-Renewal. (Summer, 13): 111-125.

[359] Arthur, W. (1989). Competing Technologies, Increasing Returns, and Lock-in by Historical Events. *Economic Journal*. 99: 116-131.

[360] Cowan, R. and Gunby, P. (1996). Sprayed to Death: Path-Dependence, Lock-in and Pest Control Strategies. *Economic Journal*. 106: 521-542.

[361] Arthur, W. (1983). Competing Technologies and Lock-in by Historical Events: The Dynamics of Allocation Under Increasing Returns. Analysis Paper WP 83-92, International Institute for Applied Systems: Laxenburg, Austria.

[362] Burgelman, R. (2002a). Strategy as Vector and the Inertia of Coevolutionary Lock-in. *Administrative Science Quarterly*: 47(2): 325-357.

[363] David, P. (1985). Clio and the economics of QUERTY. *American Economic Review*. 75: (May): 332-337.

[364] Helfat, C. (1994). Evolutionary trajectories in petroleum firm R&D. *Management Science*. 40(12): 1720-1747.

[365] Hannan, M. and Freeman, J. (1984). Structural Inertia and Organizational Change. *American Sociological Review*. 49: 149-164.

[366] Beatty, R. and Ulrich, D. (1991). Re-Energizing the Mature Organization. *Organizational Dynamics*. 20: 16-30.

[367] Markides, C. (1998). Strategic Innovation in Established Companies. *Sloan Management Review.* 39: (Spring): 31-42.

[368] Benner, M. and Tushman, M. (2003). Exploitation, Exploration, and Process Management: The Productivity Dilemma Revisited. *Academy of Management Review.* 28(2): 238-256.

[369] Henderson, R. (1993). Underinvestment and Incompetence as Responses to Radical Innovation: Evidence from Photolithographic Alignment Equipment Industry. *Rand Journal of Economics.* 24(2): 248-270.

[370] Levitt, B. and March, J. (1988). Organizational Learning. *Annual Review of Sociology.* 14: 319-340.

[371] Repenning, N. and Sterman, J. (2002). Capability Traps and Self-Confirming Attribution Errors in the Dynamics of Process Improvement. *Administrative Science Quarterly.* 47(2): 265-295.

[372] Levinthal, D. and March, J. (1993). The Myopia of Learning. *Strategic Management Journal.* 14(8): 95-112.

[373] Kogut, B. and Kulatilaka, N. (2001). Capabilities as Real Options. *Organization Science.* 12(6): 744-758.

[374] March, J. (1991). Exploration and Exploitation in Organizational Learning. *Organization Science.* 2(1): 71-87.

[375] Ghemawat, P. (1991). Commitment: The Strategy. New York: Free Press.

[376] Ghemawat, P. and Del Sol, P. (1998). Commitment Versus Flexibility. *California Management Review.* 40(4): 26-42.

[377] Bercovitz, J., de Figueiredo, J., and Teece, D. (1996). Firm Capabilities and Managerial Decision-Making: A Theory of Innovation Biases. In Innovation: Oversights and Foresights, Garud R, Nayyar P, Shapira Z (eds). Cambridge: Cambridge University Press, 233-259.

[378] Winter, S. (2003). Understanding Dynamic Capabilities. *Strategic Management Journal.* 24(10): 991-995.

[379] Gilbert, C. (2005). Unbundling the Structure of Inertia: Resource Versus Routine Rigidity. *Academy of Management Journal.* 48(5): 741-763.

[380] Morgan, N., Vorhies, D., and Mason, C. (2009). Marketing Orientation, Marketing Capabilities and Firm Performance. *Strategic Management Journal.* 30: 909-920.

[381] Eisenhardt, M. and Martin, J. (2000). Dynamic Capabilities: What Are They? *Strategic Management Journal.* October–November, Special Issue. 21: 1105-1121.

[382] Makadok, R. (2001). Toward a Synthesis of the Resource-Based and Dynamic-Capability Views of Rent Creation. *Strategic Management Journal.* 22(5): 387-401.

[383] Teece, D., Pisano, G., and Shuen, A. (1997). Dynamic Capabilities and Strategic Management. *Strategic Management Journal.* 18(7): 509-535.

[384] Grant, R. (1996). Prospering in Dynamically Competitive Environments: Organizational Capability as Knowledge Integration. *Organization Science.* 7(4): 375-387.

[385] Bingham, C., Eisenhardt, K., and Furr, N. (2007). What Makes a Process a Capability? Heuristics, Strategy, and Effective Capture of Opportunities. *Strategic Entrepreneurship Journal.* 1(1-2): 27-47.

[386] Ethiraj, S., Kale, P., Krishnan, M., and Singh, J. (2005). Where Do Capabilities Come from and How Do They Matter? A Study in the Software Services Industry. *Strategic Management Journal.* 26(1): 25-45.

[387] Teece, D., Pisano, G., and Shuen, A. (1997). Dynamic Capabilities and Strategic Management. *Strategic Management Journal,* 18(7): 509-535.

[388] Teece, D. (2007). Explicating Dynamic Capabilities: The Nature and Micro-Foundations of (Sustainable) Enterprise Performance. *Strategic Management Journal.* 28(13): 1319-1350.

[389] Helfat, C. (1997). Know-How and Asset Complementarity and Dynamic Capability Accumulation: The Case of R&D. *Strategic Management Journal.* 18(5): 339-360.

[390] Kohli, A. and Jaworski, B. (1990). Market Orientation: The Construct, Research Propositions and Managerial Implications. *Journal of Marketing.* 54(2): 1-18.

[391] Hult, G. and Ketchen, D. (2001). Does Market Orientation Matter? A Test of the Relationship Between Positional Advantage and Performance. *Strategic Management Journal.* 22(9): 899-906.

[392] Jaworski, B. and Kohli, A. (1993). Market Orientation: Antecedents and Consequences. *Journal of Marketing.* 57(3): 53-70.

[393] Slater, S. and Narver, J. (1995). Market Orientation and the Learning Organization. *Journal of Marketing.* 59(3): 63-74.

[394] Eisenhardt, M. and Martin, J. (2000). Dynamic Capabilities: What Are They? *Strategic Management Journal.* October–November, Special Issue, 21: 1105-1121.

[395] Danneels, E. (2007). The Process of Technological Competence Leveraging. *Strategic Management Journal.* 28(5): 511-533.

[396] Dutta, S., Zbaracki, M. and Bergen, M. (2003). Pricing Process as a Capability: A Resource-Based Perspective. *Strategic Management Journal.* 24(7): 615-630.

[397] Vorhies, D. and Morgan, N. (2005). Benchmarking Marketing Capabilities for Sustained Competitive Advantage. *Journal of Marketing.* 69(1): 80-94.

[398] Morgan, N., Zou, S., Vorhies, D., and Katsikeas, C. (2003). Experiential and Informational Knowledge, Architectural Marketing Capabilities, and the Adaptive Performance of Export Ventures. *Decision Sciences.* 34(2): 287-321.

[399] Hult, G. and Ketchen, D., (2001). Does Market Orientation Matter? A Test of the Relationship Between Positional Advantage and Performance. *Strategic Management Journal.* 22(9): 899-906.

[400] Dutta, S., Zbaracki, M., and Bergen, M. (2003). Pricing Process as a Capability: A Resource-Based Perspective. *Strategic Management Journal.* 24(7): 615-630

[401] Vorhies, D. and Morgan, N. (2005). Benchmarking Marketing Capabilities for Sustained Competitive Advantage. *Journal of Marketing.* 69(1): 80-94.

[402] Teece, D. (2007). Explicating Dynamic Capabilities: The Nature and Micro-Foundations of (Sustainable) Enterprise Performance. *Strategic Management Journal.* 28(13): 1319-1350.

[403] Grant, R. (1996). Prospering in Dynamically Competitive Environments: Organizational Capability as Knowledge Integration. *Organization Science.* 7(4): 375-387.

[404] Day, G. (1994). The Capabilities of Market-Driven Organizations. *Journal of Marketing*, 58(4): 37-51.

[405] Eisenhardt, M. and Martin, J. (2000). Dynamic Capabilities: What Are They? *Strategic Management Journal.* October–November, Special Issue. 21: 1105-1121.

[406] Danneels, E. (2007). The Process of Technological Competence Leveraging. *Strategic Management Journal.* 28(5): 511-533.

[407] Helfat, C. (1997). Know-How and Asset Complementarity and Dynamic Capability Accumulation: The Case of R&D. *Strategic Management Journal.* 18(5): 339-360.

[408] Madhavan, R. and Grover, R. (1998). From Embedded to Embodied Knowledge: New Product Development as Knowledge Management. *Journal of Marketing.* 62(4): 1-12.

[409] Makadok, R. (2001). Toward a Synthesis of the Resource-Based and Dynamic-Capability Views of Rent Creation. *Strategic Management Journal.* 22(5): 387–401.

[410] Day, G. (1994). The Capabilities of Market-Driven Organizations. *Journal of Marketing*. 58(4): 37-51.

[411] Teece, D. (2007). Explicating Dynamic Capabilities: The Nature and Micro-Foundations of (Sustainable) Enterprise Performance. *Strategic Management Journal*. 28(13): 1319-1350.

[412] Reed, R. and Defillipi, R. (1990). Causal Ambiguity, Barriers to Imitation, and Sustainable Competitive Advantage. *Academy of Management Review*. 15(1): 88-102.

[413] Helfat, C. (1997). Know-How and Asset Complementarity and Dynamic Capability Accumulation: The Case of R&D. *Strategic Management Journal*. 18(5): 339-360.

[414] Madhavan, R. and Grover, R. (1998). From Embedded to Embodied Knowledge: New Product Development as Knowledge Management. *Journal of Marketing*. 62(4): 1-12.

[415] Dobni, C. and Luffman, G. (2003). Determining the Scope and Impact of Market Orientation Profiles on Strategy Implementation and Performance. *Strategic Management Journal*. 24(6): 577-585.

[416] Ketchen, D., Hult, G., and Slater, S. (2007). Toward Greater Understanding of Market Orientation and the Resource-Based View. *Strategic Management Journal*. 28(9): 961-964.

[417] Morgan, N., Vorhies, D., and Mason, C. (2009). Marketing Orientation, Marketing Capabilities and Firm Performance. *Strategic Management Journal*. 30: 909-920.

[418] Ibid.

[419] Kirca A., Jayachandran, S., and Bearden, W. (2005). Market Orientation: A Meta-Analytic Review and Assessment of its Antecedents and Impact on Performance. *Journal of Marketing*. 69(2): 24-41.

[420] Newbert, S. (2007). Empirical Research on the Resource-Based view of the firm: An Assessment and Suggestions for Future Research. *Strategic Management Journal*. 28(2): 121-146.

[421] Teece, D. (2007). Explicating Dynamic Capabilities: The Nature and Micro-Foundations of (Sustainable) Enterprise Performance. *Strategic Management Journal*. 28(13): 1319-1350.

[422] Eisenhardt, M. and Martin, J. (2000). Dynamic Capabilities: What Are They? *Strategic Management Journal*. October–November, Special Issue, 21: 1105-1121.

CHAPTER
EIGHT

To put a spin on a common phrase, demographic *diversity* is destiny. The U.S. multicultural population is the fastest growing segment of the U.S. population.[423] Already more than 120 million strong and increasing by 2.3 million per year, [424] the U.S. multicultural population is indisputably the growth engine for leading corporations, today and in the future. Latinos, African Americans, Asians and all other multicultural consumers make up close to 40 percent of the U.S. population, with the U.S. Census projecting that they will become a majority by 2043.[425]

Today, some of the largest cities in the United States are driven by the multicultural population. New York is 68 percent multicultural.[426] Chicago, 70 percent.[427] Dallas, 71 percent. [428] Los Angeles, 73 percent.[429] Miami, 90 percent.[430] Hawaii, California, Nevada, New Mexico, Texas, and Maryland are all multicultural majority states.[431] And nationwide, there are almost 300 counties (as of 2019) where the majority of the population is multicultural.[432] The stark reality of a shifting demographic is here. Right now. It's not a futuristic phenomenon. It is a reality that impacts our country, our communities and commerce, from large corporations to small mom and pops.

The United States will be shaped and influenced by its growing multiculturalism. According to Census projections, Latinos will account for more than 50 percent of all U.S. population growth by 2020 and 85 percent by 2050.[433] African American growth will accelerate to 18 percent of total population growth by 2020 and increase to 21 percent by 2050, while Asian Americans will be responsible for 15 percent of total growth by 2020 and increase to 19 percent by 2050.[434] Non-Latino Whites, on the other hand, are projected to decline by 6 percent in 2030, by 29 percent in 2040, and by 39 percent in 2050.[435]

Today, virtually all marketers are aware of these seismic shifts. The key to unlocking growth opportunities – at the brand level – is couched in the following question: How can corporate America drive growth in a multicultural America?

I have attempted to answer this question using the traditional Resource-Based View. Currently a dominant view of business strategy, the Resource-Based View is based on the notion that a firm is a collection of unique capabilities.[436] Traditional strategy models, such as the Five Forces Model, focus on a company's external competitive environment and do not attempt to look within the firm.[437] The Resource-Based view, in contrast, highlights the need for a fit between the external market context and a firm's internal capabilities.

The Resource-Based View is grounded in the perspective that a firm's resources and capabilities are more important to strategy than its external environment. Instead of focusing on the accumulation of resources necessary to implement strategy dictated by the constraints imposed by the external environment, the Resource-Based View suggests that a firm's unique internal resources and capabilities provide the basis *for* strategy. The strategy chosen should allow the firm to best exploit its core competencies relative to opportunities in the external environment.[438] A sustainable competitive advantage is, therefore, achieved by continuously developing existing resources and capabilities and by creating new ones, in response to rapidly changing market conditions.

In this book, I have proposed that corporations must develop a new set of capabilities to drive strategy in an increasingly diverse America. If they do not adapt, they will die (a slow death). Their competition, which at some point will address the changing landscape more effectively and efficiently, will take their business. These capabilities are based on two key competencies: (1) hiring and developing multicultural marketing specialists who are also subject-matter experts in key disciplines (i.e., strategy, media, technology, etc.) and (2) developing a corporate culture that reflects a 21st-century America. Companies that challenge the status quo and their ethnocentrism will have the opportunity to better understand their evolving consumer.

Internal processes will need to reflect the New Mainstream. This means building a strategic process that leads with Latino and African American consumer insights, from creating a strategy, to developing inclusive creative briefs, to measuring the impact of campaigns across target segments. Inclusive and diverse at its core, this new form of "total market" that leads with the multicultural population will become the de facto marketing standard in the 21st century. When embraced, this approach will supersede all other marketing practices and become the new marketing paradigm.

So how do clients move toward this new reality? To answer this question, I have outlined a 2x2 model based on four quadrants that will guide the advertising and marketing industry through the evolution (or steps) necessary to win in a diverse marketplace. Quadrants One and Two represent a starting point for many entrants in multicultural marketing whereas Quadrants

Three and Four are fertile spaces for companies with a bit more experience in marketing in a multicultural America.

In Chapter 4, I introduced the Four-Quadrant Model of Cultural Marketing, which helps explain the evolution of marketing communications in detail. The model features four quadrants based on two variables, language and consumer insights. The language axis is operationalized in two ways: Spanish and English. The consumer insights axis is comprised of two dimensions, mainstream and multicultural. While the marketplace is dynamic and complex, and a 2x2 matrix has its limitations, the proposed model is nevertheless robust in capturing the nuances of consumers and the various marketing approaches in the United States. Marketing strategy needs to be analyzed by the climate in which it is created, by the people who create it and by the political and business forces that shape it. The 2x2 framework yields powerful actionable insights for brands.

Quadrant One encompasses clients and advertising agencies with the least amount of expertise in targeting multicultural consumers. A client in Quadrant One is likely to think about the multicultural consumer after developing their general market strategy. The outcome may look like a general market strategy (or execution) that is literally translated to reach Latinos or Asian consumers. Quadrant Two is based on the adaptation of the general market approach, often based on a singular strategy, but with different executions to address cultural nuances. Quadrant Three is the closest to executing a pure segmentation approach, with an original strategy and execution for different multicultural consumers. These consumers are not effectively reached by English-language media. Quadrant Four is based on a strategy developed and executed for a multicultural audience in English.

Given the demographic changes in our country, Quadrant Four will redefine mainstream marketing, as we know it.

I should point out that no single approach will satisfy all client objectives. The "one-size-fits-all" total market approach is a panacea. To drive maximum growth, I have suggested that companies align with Quadrants Three and Four. The fundamental question for brands is: Which segments are responsible for driving volume and growth? Those are the segments that need to be prioritized. Moving forward, it is unthinkable that the multicultural population will continue to be relegated to a segmentation strategy when they represent more than 65 percent of the total population in the majority of America's big cities. Corporations will need to be more effective in measuring and attributing sales to specific multicultural consumers. The solution will require companies to develop customized analytic models that address their marketing mix. The proposed 2x2 matrix can help brands actively manage their trajectory and understand what they need to do to win with different ethnic and racial consumers, including non-Latino Whites.

The billion-dollar question is: What does marketing look like in the future? Culture is the common denominator in a multicultural America, and marketing in the 21st century is multicultural at its core. The popular in-culture marketing approach will continue to support brands in the in-language vertical and brands will rightsize their investments in this silo. More companies will learn that their core customers are multicultural, and consumer insights will be led by Latino and African American consumers.

Based on my 30 year career in the advertising and marketing industry, I want to leave you with what I'm calling the "Ten marketing rules to winning in a multicultural America." You can think of them as best practices.

10 Beware of false prophets and marketing practices "du jour."

9 Build a learning organization.

8 Build dynamic capabilities for your firm.

7 Build an organization of the 21st century.

6 Integration will enable business growth.

5 Measure what matters with granularity.

4 Kill ethnocentrism at all cost.

3 Love and listen to thy customer.

2 The New Mainstream is multicultural.

1 Marketing starts and ends with the customer.

In closing, developing and implementing strategy for the New Mainstream is relatively easy, compared to the work that is required to reinvent the culture of an organization rooted in the 20th century. As you think about your company's path to success, I end this book with the following Hindi adage: "As your deed is, so is your destiny."

Is your company ready to make The Big Shift?

CHAPTER EIGHT ENDNOTES

[423] U.S. Census Bureau, 2020.

[424] Ibid.

[425] Ibid.

[426] Ibid.

[427] Ibid.

[428] Ibid.

[429] Ibid.

[430] Ibid.

[431] Ibid.

[432] Krogstad, J. (2019). Reflecting a Demographic Shift, 109 U.S. Counties Have Become Majority Nonwhite Since 2000. Pew Research Center. Accessed on: https://www.pewresearch.org/fact-tank/2019/08/21/u-s-counties-majority-nonwhite/

[433] U.S. Census Bureau, Projections.

[434] Ibid.

[435] Ibid.

[436] Barney, J. (1991). Firm Resources and Sustained Competitive Advantage. *Journal of Management*. 17(1): 99-120.

[437] Porter, M. (1985). The Competitive Advantage: Creating and Sustaining Superior Performance. New York: Free Press.

[438] Hansen, G. and Wernerfelt, B. (1989). Determinants of Firm Performance: The Relative Importance of Economic and Organizational Factors. *Strategic Management Journal*. 10(5): 399-411.

CPSIA information can be obtained
at www.ICGtesting.com
Printed in the USA
FSHW021304070521
81236FS

9 781647 042233